# PRAISE FOR *A MARKED HEART*

"Martin Luther King, Jr. inspired David George Ball to find his true calling – in public service."

– Liz Humes, Wordy Bird, WRIR-FM (Richmond, VA)

"Ball's tale is one of sincerity and struggle. . . A worthy life. . ."

- *Kirkus Indie*

"David George Ball came to America in 1954 as a teenager to follow his father into the ministry. An encounter with another minister, Martin Luther King,, Jr., led him into public service where he championed the expansion of the 401(k) program.  Today more than 70 million workers have 401(k) plans."

 - *The Virginia Gazette*

"From UK school to US politics"

- *The Citizen*, Gloucester, England

"An amazing story"

–*Virginia This Morning*, WTVR-TV (CBS Affiliate)

"One man can change the lives of millions. *A Marked Heart* is the story of one of those millions.  David George Ball was pursuing becoming a pastor, but his meeting with Dr. Martin Luther Kings, Jr. sent him in another path of helping people, as a lawyer and politician. Telling of his journey through these careers and how God and Dr. King did much in his path, *A Marked Heart* is a poignant and thoughtful read, very much recommended."

– James Cox, *Midwest Book Review*

"An inspiring tale of how one person can truly make a difference"

- Elizabeth Dole, U.S. Senator 2003-2009,
Secretary of Labor 1989 – 1990

"This is a deeply moving memoir of a young man, who came from England to Moody to take the pastors' course, and went on to outstanding public service! *A Marked Heart* reminds all of us where to look for help in coping with the conflicts and pressures in our lives."

– Marvin E. Beckman,
General Counsel 1970 – 2006
Moody Bible Institute

"A heart-warming portrait of faith, pushing back against adversity, in an amazing journey inspired by Martin Luther King."

- The Right Reverend Herman Hollerith IV
Bishop of the Diocese of Southern Virginia Episcopal Church

*To Bob and Esther*

# A Marked Heart

*Blessings*

## David George Ball

*David George Ball*

iUniverse, Inc.
Bloomington

# A Marked Heart

The views expressed in this work are solely those of the author and do not necessarily reflect the views of the publisher, and the publisher hereby disclaims any responsibility for them.

iUniverse books may be ordered through booksellers or by contacting:

iUniverse
1663 Liberty Drive
Bloomington, IN 47403
www.iuniverse.com
1-800-Authors (1-800-288-4677)

Because of the dynamic nature of the Internet, any web addresses or links contained in this book may have changed since publication and may no longer be valid.

Any people depicted in stock imagery provided by Thinkstock are models, and such images are being used for illustrative purposes only.

Certain stock imagery © Thinkstock.

ISBN: 978-1-4620-0214-6 (sc)
ISBN: 978-1-4620-0216-0 (dj)
ISBN: 978-1-4620-0215-3 (ebk)

Library of Congress Control Number: 2011903168

Printed in the United States of America

iUniverse rev. date: 10/6/2011

*"Congratulations on your excellent service as Assistant Secretary for Pension and Welfare Benefits under President Bush. You should be proud of your success in strengthening the integrity of the private pension system."*
—Letter from President Gerald R. Ford

# Contents

*To Carol, David Jr., Christopher, Deborah,
Jonathan, and Thomas, with love.*

# Introduction

In looking back, I understand now what an incredible force my missionary mother was in my life. As a child in wartime England, I thought she was just like everybody else's mother. Although she frequently reminded me she had dedicated me to the Lord's service, at first I didn't grasp what she meant. Gradually I began to realize she was different. She seemed to think her will and God's will were the same. If I didn't obey her, I wasn't pleasing the Lord.

After I was accepted for the pastors' course at Moody Bible Institute in Chicago, my mother moved the family to America to keep an eye on me. As a seventeen-year-old immigrant, I had no idea that an encounter with Martin Luther King Jr. would help free me from the rigid course she had decreed. I had never met a black person before I came to America. But those three days with Dr. King as my guest at Yale changed the direction of my life forever. I switched my major to politics and decided to go to law school.

Inspired by King's example, I dreamed of making a positive difference in people's lives. However, my new career didn't make my life any easier. In fact it became more difficult than when I was dealing with my mother. Instead of the ministry, my quest led me to the rigors of a Wall Street law firm.

Seven years later, my political journey came to an abrupt halt when my beloved wife died, leaving me with three young children. In the first terrible months after that tragedy, I desperately needed my mother's help and support. I also found comfort in the story of Job in the Bible and in prayer. In time I found another wonderful partner and stepmother for my children.

Eventually my career took off again as an officer of a large metals and mining company. But over the years, ambition undermined my faith and my family life. This is an insider's true story of the price executives often pay for getting ahead.

When the metals business turned down, I devised a radical plan to reduce corporate debt and help the company survive. Instead of rewarding me with a promotion, a new cutthroat chief executive kicked me out. Once again I found refuge in prayer and was given the opportunity to make a new beginning in public service.

My goal in writing this book is to give readers a perspective on some of the questions many of us ask: Can we make a difference in the world? Where do we turn in a crisis? How do we deal with too much ambition? I hope my story will prove helpful as readers confront the pressures and conflicts in their own lives.

# Chapter One

## *IRENE AND HAROLD*

Before she married my father, my mother—whose maiden name was Irene Hadley—was a missionary. She never explained what gave her the steely determination, when she was sixteen, to abandon her carefree life as the eldest daughter of a prosperous corn merchant in Gloucester, England, for a job teaching deaf and dumb children in London. But apparently, she wanted to get as far away as possible from her family. As soon as she was twenty-one and legally free to decide for herself, she volunteered to serve with the Lakher Pioneer Mission in a remote part of the British Empire in India, near the border with Nepal.

In 1928 she sailed through the Suez Canal to Calcutta and traveled north by boat, canoe, and on foot along goat paths to a tribe of former headhunters in the foothills of the Himalayas. She worked in a bamboo church teaching young girls personal hygiene, handicrafts, and the Christian gospel.

Years later she delighted in telling me how she discovered a naked boy crying in a clay pot in the dense vegetation at the side of the path to her bungalow. She grabbed the baby and ran to look for the head missionary. "Look who I've found."

The cautious older missionary seemed taken aback. "That's what the Lakhers do with babies when their mother dies in childbirth."

But Mum persisted. "The Lord wants me to take the place of his mother."

I heard a lot about this little fellow whom she named Peter after her brother in Australia. He slept in her bedroom. She couldn't get enough cow or goat milk for him so she chewed up rice to pass with her mouth. One night as he lay contented on the bed with milk dripping down his chin, a large snake slithered into her room. She killed it with a rake.

Life in the rain forest was tough. Mosquitoes got inside the tattered netting over her bed and she caught malaria. As the years passed, her teeth rotted. Another missionary pulled them out with pliers.

Seven years later, Irene left Peter with the other missionaries and returned to England on furlough. She was emaciated and suffering from the recurrent malaria that was to plague her off and on for the rest of her life. She planned to remain in Gloucester for a few months to train as a midwife so she could help the Lakher women with childbirth. In Gloucester she was fitted with false teeth, but her poor health made her dread going back. She couldn't admit to anyone how she felt.

A friend told her about Trinity Baptist Church, a new chapel in a development of concrete council houses called the "White City." The next Sunday morning Irene cycled to this mission field of poor families. Over a hundred needy souls gathered in a temporary building to hear the good-looking, muscular, young preacher named Harold Ball proclaim the gospel. On that fateful day after the service she shook his hand and offered to help.

Since Harold rented a room on Calton Road not far from Tuffley Avenue where she lived, they cycled home together. According to Dad, when they reached her home she continued to ask questions about the work at Trinity. For his part he was impressed. Miss Hadley came from The Lawn, a gentleman's house. He was just a farm boy.

Harold's dearest childhood memory was pleasing his mother. She liked him to rub her back when she was tired from farm chores and caring for her family of six. In the epidemic at the end of the Great War in 1918, his mother caught the Spanish Flu. Eleven-year-old Harold lay awake listening to her cough and moan with pain. He prayed, "I'll be ever so good, God, if you let Mother get better."

One night he awoke to silence. In the morning a neighbor asked, "How's your mother today?"

Harold had to say the black words, "She died."

Farmer neighbors pulled the hearse up the road to Thornbury cemetery. Harold and his nine-year-old brother followed on either side of their father holding his hands. His two younger sisters stayed at home.

His father hired a housekeeper named Miss Pitt. She was an upright Christian who kept the house straight and got food on the table. But she gave the children no birthday parties and no warmth. On the Lord's Day, after milking, his father took them to Sunday school and chapel.

As a teenager, Harold drove the horse and cart with the milk churns to Thornbury Station in time for the eight o'clock train to Bristol. Then he drove back to Oak Farm, turned the horse out to graze, and cycled to school in Thornbury. After school he helped his father milk their herd of cows. At age sixteen he started as an apprentice on a farm in Charfield.

Dad said this was a turning point in his life. He heard a sermon in the local chapel about the second coming of Christ. He shuddered because he had no assurance of his salvation. That night after he blew out the candle, he knelt beside his bed. He prayed with the words of a hymn, "My Jesus, I love Thee, I . . ." but he stopped, unable to finish the sentence. In the darkness he begged, "Lord, help me finish that line." Suddenly, it seemed as if the light of heaven flooded his soul and he cried out, "My Jesus, I love Thee, I *know* Thou art mine." For the rest of his life he never doubted God's presence.

He began to preach in country chapels and decided to train for the ministry. I've heard him say a thousand times, "Farming was in my blood, but preaching was in my heart!"

His father admired the American evangelist Dwight Moody, who held legendary revival meetings in England in the 1870s. He suggested Harold consider attending the school called Moody Bible Institute, which the evangelist founded in Chicago. The idea of going to America thrilled Harold. He sailed for New York at Christmas in 1927.

Despite working long hours as a waiter at Marshall Field's to meet his living expenses, he embraced Moody and America. He became student pastor of a church in the suburbs of Chicago. He used to tell me, "It's a land flowing with milk and honey." His enthusiasm made me wish I could go to America too.

After returning to England, for two years he devoted his energy to a church in a poor area of London. In 1932, he received a call to Trinity Baptist Church in Gloucester.

Dad always chuckled when he told me what happened after that young missionary showed up at the morning service. The very next day she arrived at his lodging with many practical ideas as to how she could help the cause at Trinity. She said, "I want to double the attendance."

Dad put her in charge of the primary Sunday school and the children's Band of Hope. Soon she gave him an intriguing token of their friendship—a wall plaque that carried a text from the Bible: "If God be for us, who can be against us?" Unsure what to make of the gift, he hung it in his bedroom. She told him she had another plaque that she would give him sometime. He wondered what it said, but she admonished him. "Wait and see."

The next time she visited his lodging, she dropped a hint. "I think we make a great team at Trinity."

He didn't know quite how to answer but managed, "You certainly are helpful to me in my ministry."

A few weeks later Irene was more direct. "Harold, I believe it's the Lord's will for us to be married."

He swallowed and looked down.

She continued. "I'm going to pray about it!" and sped off on her bike like a post office messenger who had just delivered a telegram.

After she left he realized he felt overwhelmed and excited that someone wanted him. She seemed so self-assured, so confident. A dedicated Christian and a hard worker, she would make a good minister's wife. As the weeks went by he came to believe the Lord had sent her to him. They decided to get married at Trinity on January 14, 1936.

I have often studied the photograph taken at The Lawn after their wedding for clues about Mum. The grass glistened white with hoarfrost. Harold stood almost six feet tall with square shoulders and a serious, handsome face. Irene, with her sparkling brown eyes and radiant smile, had found in him an honorable way not to return to Lakherland. Slender and healthy again and all of five feet four inches in height, she clasped his arm decisively.

*Harold, Irene and wedding party in garden at the Lawn on January 14, 1936. Bridesmaids from left, Peggy Hadley, Joan Hadley and Doris Ball*

They laughed when she produced the other plaque. It said, "As for me and my house, we will serve the Lord." He was flattered that she had marriage in mind all along. It came as no surprise that I was born less than a year later, on November 16, 1936.

At first we lived in a rented house, but a few months later Irene's mother, whom I would learn to call Granny Hadley, helped them buy a house of their own. Squeezed into a narrow lot with a few windows back and front, it stood modestly in a row of identical drab brick houses on Lewisham Road.

When I was one month old, Dad conducted my dedication service at chapel, just as he would for the parents of any child born to a member of his congregation. On behalf of himself and Mum, he prayed for grace to bring me up in a Christian home, so that once I reached the age of discretion, I would choose to be baptized and join the church.

But Mum had an additional agenda. With all the force of her dominating personality, she tapped me for the ministry. Just as Abraham bound Isaac his son and laid him on the altar, so she offered me. Like Isaac, I was not in a position to make the decision myself. Mum heard God tell her what to do. From then on, I was a marked man.

The story that follows describes my struggle to affirm my true self.

# Chapter Two

## *Childhood in Wartime England*

On a summer day in 1939 when I'm almost three, Mum takes my one-year-old brother, Jonathan, and me on the green double-decker Calton Road bus to visit her sister, Joyce, and my cousins Jeremy and Jane on the posh side of Gloucester. She stops at a dairy to buy ice cream. She must want to please Auntie Joyce, because Mum can't afford ice cream for us. As Auntie slices the frozen block on the kitchen table, they talk about Uncle Cyril, who is an architect and has drawn up plans for a new building at Dad's church.

The next time we visit Auntie Joyce, the dairy has stopped making ice cream. Mum says, "It's because of the war."

Soon after I begin Calton Road Primary School on my third birthday, I arrive home to find Mum and Dad cutting up large strips of black paper in the front room. Mum explains, "We have to black out all the windows so the German planes can't see us at night." Dad doesn't have enough black paper for the front window of our brick row house so Mum tells him to use a poster with a verse from the Bible: "God is our refuge and strength, a very present help in trouble." People passing by say they find it comforting.

On Christmas morning Mum tells me to put on my best clothes and we walk over to The Lawn, the big house where my grandparents live. Mum's father, Grandpa Hadley, instructs us to wait in the hall for Father Christmas and disappears into the kitchen. A loud knock makes Granny open the front door. Father Christmas stands laughing on the doorstep with a strange white beard, a floppy red hat, and a large red dressing gown. He has glasses on the end of his nose, just like Grandpa. He says, "Ho, ho, ho! Who are you?"

*David and Jonathan in front of their home in Gloucester, England, in 1940. The text in the window says, "God is our refuge and strength, a very present help in trouble."*

"David."

"Who's that?"

"My brother, Jonathan."

"Well, that's lucky." He hands us several packages wrapped in shiny red paper.

Grandpa Hadley returns from the kitchen to watch us open our presents. This is the last time I see him, but the magical memory of my kindly Father Christmas stays with me forever.

A few weeks later, I awake to find the iron railings in front of our house and all the other houses in the row have been ripped away. One of our neighbors complains to Dad. "Nobody asked permission to take the railings, and nobody paid for them!"

Dad doesn't like to see them gone either, but says stoically, "They'll be melted down to build tanks."

At Calton Road Primary School, my teacher, Miss Morgan, hands out cardboard boxes. She says the boxes contain masks to protect us if the Germans use mustard gas. My mask is rubber with a small, round cylinder in front of the mouth and goggles for the eyes. The mouthpiece pinches my chin. Miss Morgan tightens the buckle at the back of my head, and I feel trapped inside a small, dimly lit room. She tells me to breathe normally. She must be kidding because I can't help but breathe fast. I'm smothering. The other members of the class bob around, but I can't see them very well.

Finally, Miss Morgan tells us to take off the masks and put them back in the boxes. She says, "When the air raid siren goes off, line up at the door in pairs with your gas masks." I wonder what an air raid siren sounds like. She keeps going over to the window to listen, but nothing happens. At the end of class she tells us to take the gas masks home with us in case we need them at night. From then on, I take my gas mask to and from school every day.

The following week we hear a loud whining in the distance. It must be the air raid siren. Miss Morgan says, "Stand in line and no talking." We walk to the playing field carrying our cardboard boxes. There are four large barrage balloons way up in the sky and tethered to stakes in the corner of the playing field. They are supposed to stop German planes from flying low over Gloucester.

Somebody has dug huge holes at the edge of the fields, covered the holes with corrugated iron, piled dirt on top, surrounded the entrances with sandbags, and created mysterious caves in the ground. Miss Morgan tells us to step down into the air raid shelter. We sit on a bench and put on our gas masks. There are several other teachers inside the shelter with their pupils. It is dark and scary. We stay there until we hear the all-clear siren.

Mum takes Jonathan and me to Sunday school. She keeps everyone spellbound by acting out the Bible stories and teaching us to use our hands and arms as we sing choruses about the Savior's love. Because she always tells me what to do, I feel safe. I don't know yet about her ferocious determination to make me a minister.

On the spur of the moment in early spring, Mum shows us the tennis court at the bottom of the garden at The Lawn. The close-cut grass is freshly marked with white lines. I ask, "What are those for?"

"You must keep the ball inside the lines."

"Did you really play tennis here?"

"Yes, with Auntie Joyce."

"Can we play?"

"No, the equipment is put away in the summer house."

I run over to look in the window. Mum jerks me away and snaps, "Don't go in there!" Her face colors. She rushes us off and never takes us back. I wonder why the summer house made her cross. It will be many years before I discover it is connected to a family secret.

In May 1940 Dad listens to the news on the BBC. It sounds bad. The German army has overrun Holland and Belgium and swept into France. A few days later three hundred thousand soldiers are evacuated from Dunkirk. I see a picture in the newspaper of the new prime minister, Winston Churchill, giving a defiant V-for-victory sign. He says on the radio, "We shall go on to the end … whatever the cost may be, we shall fight on the beaches, we shall fight on the landing-grounds, we shall fight in the fields and in the streets, we shall fight in the hills; we shall never surrender!"

When I hear about the prime minister, I think Dad must be important because he's a minister too, but the BBC never mentions him. He runs all the meetings at chapel and spends a lot of time visiting people in their homes. He serves as chaplain to the soldiers at the Reservoir Road Army Camp. What's more, he also ministers to men arriving in ambulances at Gloucester hospital. They come for plastic surgery to replace noses and ears blown off in the fighting.

Dad says, "Those brave young pilots were shot down in the Battle of Britain. They stopped the invasion!"

Dad has enlisted in the Royal Observer Corps. Twice a week at night after his other jobs, he puts on his uniform and reports to the headquarters in downtown Gloucester. I ask, "What do you do at the Observer Corps?"

He explains, "We get phone calls from plane spotters on the south coast who watch for German planes coming across the English Channel."

"What do you do about it?"

"We report to RAF Fighter Command so they can shoot down the planes."

One evening while I put on my pajamas, he cautions, "If you hear the air raid siren, you must turn off your bedroom light. I may be on air raid duty."

Before long I hear the siren howling up and down like a sick dog. I quickly plunge Jonathan and myself into darkness and scramble under the bed. Jonathan copies me. Hundreds of heavy bombers thunder over our house. They're coming here, right into the bedroom! The window starts to shiver and shake.

Through a crack at the side of the blackout paper I see a searchlight sweeping the sky. An ack-ack gun at Staverton airport rattles in desperation. I freeze stiff until I hear the long steady "all clear." I hope Dad isn't getting bombed.

At breakfast I tell Mum I crawled under the bed. She says firmly, "You don't need to do that. You must be brave!" Mum doesn't seem to be afraid. I mustn't show that I am.

The next night the terrifying bombers thunder over our house again. I pull the sheets over my head and try not to think about them. Tomorrow I will be four years old.

In the morning I hear Dad talking to Mum in the kitchen in a low voice. Some words slip out, "Coventry cathedral ... ruins." Mum and Dad seem to have forgotten about my birthday.

Some government workmen come to our house with metal beams and a square of steel. They build a small air raid shelter right in the middle of our tiny dining room. Mum puts a tablecloth over the top, and we use it as our dining room table. It seems funny eating beans on toast on top of an air raid shelter.

In the beginning, when the siren howls, we all crawl into the steel cage. It's a tight fit with Mum, Dad, Jonathan, and me. After a while, I notice we just carry on with dinner. I ask, "Why don't we crawl under the table anymore?"

"The Germans aren't going to bomb here," Mum replies. "They want to destroy the factories up north."

But they do bomb us after all. As I walk home from school with Dad and Jonathan, I hear a plane flying over the center of town. There's no air raid siren. Dad yells, "A German plane!" I see three bombs dropping. *Boom! Boom! Boom!* The ground trembles. Dad grabs our hands and we run back to our dining room bomb shelter. Mum crawls in too.

Later on, Dad says one bomb hit near the railroad station, another destroyed Elim Church, and the third wiped out some houses in Park Road only a mile away. I wonder if there were any people in those houses.

In another sneak attack, a bomb hits the gate of the aircraft factory that builds the Gloster Spitfire—a fighter plane used in the war. I hear the bomb killed a bus driver waiting to pick up workers on their way home. Mum and Dad won't tell me any more details.

I blurt out to my friend Howard at school about the bus driver. He stares back at me. "People are getting bombed to death all over England."

I'm scared, but I know I mustn't say.

Two weeks before Christmas 1940, someone comes to the house with a message. Dad takes me to the place on Calton Road where he had rented a room on coming to Gloucester. His former landlady tells him she saw Grandpa Hadley fall off his bike while riding past her house. She says, "He must have had a heart attack. I ran into the bakery and called the hospital."

On the way home I ask Dad, "Will Grandpa get better?"

Dad replies, "We must pray for him."

Every night when I say my prayers, I pray for Grandpa.

On Christmas day we walk over to The Lawn just as we had done last year. When we arrive Granny seems flustered. She whispers to Mum, who tells us to wait by the front door. We stand there for a very long time. Finally, someone knocks, and Mum opens the door. The metal tub that the maid uses to carry the laundry sits on the doorstep heaped with colorfully wrapped packages. There is no sign of Father Christmas, although I notice someone disappearing round the corner of the house. It could be Dad. I race to the corner but arrive too late to see who it is.

As we return home, Dad walks with me holding my hand. I ask, "Where's Grandpa?"

He replies softly, "Grandpa died this morning." My eyes blur with tears. I've lost my Father Christmas. But Mum keeps a straight face.

With tight lips she steers Jonathan and the parcels in the pushchair. I don't understand why she doesn't cry.

Back home Dad says to Mum, "At the Observer Corps we got an amazing message about a huge fleet of planes approaching from thirty miles out at sea. Usually we get no warning until the bombers fly right over the coast."

She exclaims, "There are no plane spotters in the English Channel."

"You're right," he replies. "But the message proved correct and the German planes arrived to bomb the south of England." Afterward, Dad learns we have a new invention called radio detecting and ranging, which enables us to locate incoming planes far out at sea. Later this is called radar.

Two Polish girls come down from London to live in our back bedroom. Dad explains, "They were rescued by the Christian Mission to Jews just before Hitler invaded Poland." I can't understand what they say, but I know they're glad to escape from the Blitz.

Dad mutters, "We're all alone against Hitler."

# Chapter Three

## *Young Warrior*

Soon after my fifth birthday, I play on the floor with some wooden blocks while Dad listens to the BBC. We hear President Roosevelt talking to the American Congress. "Yesterday, December 7, 1941, a date which will live in infamy, the United States of America was suddenly and deliberately attacked by the naval and air forces of the Empire of Japan."

Dad yells, "Irene. Quickly, come and listen."

The news continues, "Within four hours, Congress declared war on Japan. Germany declared war on the United States and America came in on our side."

Dad beams. He knows about America because he studied at Moody Bible Institute in Chicago. He says to Mum, "It will make all the difference!"

The Polish girls leave and American soldiers or nurses stay in our back bedroom. My favorite is Corporal Pete May. He smiles a lot. As a special privilege, Dad takes me to the evening gospel service to hear him give his testimony.

Later he sits on the edge of his bed to talk and doesn't mind my questions. "Why are you here?" I ask.

"President Roosevelt sent me over to help you win the war."

"What do you do?"

"I take apart bombs that don't explode when they land."

"Isn't that dangerous?"

He hesitates. "I try not to think about it."

"What do you do in America?"

"I run a country store in a small town in Pennsylvania. Children come in for ice cream or a Coke. Would you like to see a photo?"

He makes room next to him on the bed and produces a picture of himself with his wife standing proudly at the counter of his store, which is full of boxes filled with strange fruit.

"What are those?" I ask.

"Those are bananas and oranges. You could get them in England before the war."

America sounds like a wonderful place with all kinds of treats. We need a ration book for meat, eggs, lard, cheese, bacon, sugar, and clothes, but when Mum sends me down to the co-op for groceries, the shelves are often empty. Sometimes the butcher doesn't have any meat. We have four fowls that are supposed to lay one egg a day for each member of our family.

Our vegetables come from our garden or Dad's allotment near the railway tracks. He slices the runner beans and stores them with salt in jars in the larder to make them last through the winter.

He says, "We must grow as much food as possible in England. The German U-boats torpedo ships bringing food from the colonies."

Although America is on our side now, German planes continue to attack towns all over the country. My cousin Roger, at Kington Mead Farm, ten miles from the city of Bristol, tells me, "At night after the air raids, you can see Bristol burning."

Now that I can read, I look at the newspaper. The news is terrible—convoys sunk, bombers shot down. The Japanese have taken Singapore.

Soldiers and sailors who are on leave come to chapel in their uniforms. Everyone looks happy to be there in the warmth instead of in their rented concrete homes in the White City with their damp beds and condensation streaming down the walls. During the evening service they belt out gospel hymns with such conviction their voices can be heard all over the neighborhood.

*David, his cousin Roger, and Jonathan in the garden in 1942.*

At Harvest Festival, which is my favorite service, Dad places trestle tables in the front of the chapel. The folks from the White City don't have much money, but they bring the best produce from their tiny gardens: the largest marrows, the longest cucumbers, the reddest tomatoes, and the most luscious apples and plums. Dad adds some eggs from our fowls and some sheaves of wheat from my uncle's farm. After the service, he takes the produce to the homes of the neediest families.

Dad says, "Coal is in short supply." His salary of three pounds a week keeps one fire burning downstairs. He teaches me how to curl up old newspapers into long rolls, tie them in knots, and place them in the grate. He adds a few pieces of kindling wood and lumps of black coal from the scuttle. While I watch, he slices a piece of bread and holds it over the red glow with a toasting fork. I lean forward eagerly as the white bread turns golden brown and the scrumptious smell of hot toast fills the room.

Mum and Dad sit in their chairs on either side of the fireplace while Jonathan and I play with our wooden blocks on the linoleum floor. Mum knits sweaters and darns over the "potatoes" or holes in the heels of our worn-out woolen socks. We stay close to the fire because of the cold draft under the door.

The bitter cold gets into our bedroom, and the condensation from our breath freezes intricate patterns on the inside of the window panes. I have to undress in a great hurry. Sometimes my fingers and toes swell up with painful red chilblains. I often have an earache. Mum puts drops in my ears to heal the infection and makes me wear an embarrassing scarf over my head.

Suddenly, I get very sweaty. My face burns. Dr. Green, our family doctor, aware of an epidemic in Gloucester, tells Mum I have diphtheria. He discusses sending me to the Children's Hospital. Many of the children sent to the Children's Hospital have died, so Mum insists on keeping me at home. Dr. Green experiments with a much stronger shot of penicillin than the dosage used in the hospital. Dad sleeps on the floor with me and keeps the fire burning. In the middle of the night, I wake with a high fever. I can't breathe. In panic, I grab Dad around his neck. All of a sudden I feel deathly tired. I fall back limply. The crisis is over.

During my recovery, I look through Mum's scrapbook full of family photographs, old birthday cards, and pictures of the royal family. I particularly like the picture of little Princess Elizabeth and Princess Margaret. They must remind Mum of her two boys. Of course I've never seen them in person, but I feel as if I know them because they are on the same page as my birthday cards.

Dad tells Mum a local businessman has paid for us to take a holiday at the seaside town of Weston-super-Mare. He says, "We can take the train." He adds wistfully, "The boys could swim if only they had bathing suits."

Mum replies, "You can't get them in the shops any more. But I'll make some." She finds an old pattern and some wool, and clickety click, she goes to work. The suits look magnificent in the dining room when we try them on—red and white stripes for me, and blue for Jonathan, with straps over our shoulders.

The first time we dash into the water, the woolen costumes sink down to our knees. Fortunately, the shoulder straps prevent them falling off completely. We yank up our sagging suits and hobble back to Mum and Dad in their deck chairs. Mum says laughing, "You'd better stay on the beach."

She starts taking Jonathan and me to the evening gospel service. The streetlights are turned off, so she gives us flashlights to help find our way home in the dark. She warns us, "If you hear a plane, turn off your flashlights."

Early in 1944, Dad talks about the invasion of Italy. But the kids at school get excited about the Russian Army advancing on the Eastern Front. They run around the playground shouting, "The Reds are coming! The Reds are coming!"

While the Red Army advances, Mum makes a move at chapel. She shuts down the Band of Hope and starts a new program for children called the Young Warriors. We have the same motto as C. T. Studd, who played cricket for England but gave it up to be a missionary with the China Inland Mission. He said, "If Jesus Christ be God and died for me, then no sacrifice can be too great for me to make for him." C. T. Studd must have been pretty amazing.

At Young Warriors, Mum tells us Bible stories, like the one about Hannah, who dedicated her baby, Samuel, to the Lord. While he was still a little boy, she took him to live at the temple with a priest named Eli. One night Samuel heard God calling to him. He answered, "Speak, Lord. I am listening." From that moment Samuel gave messages to God's people. He became a special prophet of God.

In order to qualify for the Young Warrior's badge, we must memorize our motto. Mum glows when I stand to recite the words. Her hands shake as she awkwardly pins a badge on the lapel of my coat. She whispers, "When you were born, I dedicated you to the Lord's service." I don't know what she means, but I have no reason to object.

We move to a new home at 157 Finlay Road. It has a lot more windows than our narrow row house and is nearer to the chapel. Mum hangs a plaque in the living room: "As for me and my house, we will serve the Lord."

Mum sends Jonathan and me blackberry picking on Robinswood Hill, which rises behind our garden. After climbing for twenty minutes, we reach the top. Two miles away on the banks of the River Severn, we can see Gloucester Cathedral soaring majestically, gray and white, above rows of red brick tenements.

Even though we're Baptist and not Church of England, the cathedral belongs to us too. The famous east window, built in memory of the soldiers who died in the Battle of Crecy in 1344, is covered with sandbags for protection. I hope the buzz bombs crashing on London don't hit it. You can hear the buzz bombs coming. I wonder if we will have enough time to reach the air raid shelter in our garden before they land.

As we return down Stroud Road after picking blackberries for a couple of hours, I recognize the faces of two people sitting in the backseat of a black Rolls Royce. I've seen their pictures in Mum's scrapbook. I point to the car and yell, "Look, Jonathan—it's Queen Mary and Princess Margaret!" In my wild-eyed excitement, I drop the basket and the blackberries spill all over the road.

Jonathan and I have a longer walk from our new home to school, but the streets are usually deserted. Mum says, "You can take a shortcut through the alleyway over the railway tracks."

"What about kids from the White City?" I ask.

She reassures us. "Nobody is going to hurt you."

We peer down the forbidding passage. No one in sight! We venture forward, cautiously looking all around. As we turn the first corner we hear a shout. We break into a run. Breathing hard, we make it safely across the two bridges over the railway and head downhill for Stroud Road and safety. Almost there!

At the bottom of the alley, some boys from the White City block the way. One of them grabs my arm.

I protest, "Let me go! My dad's a policeman."

"No he's not," another boy yells. "He's the minister at the chapel!"

They let us pass. I'm glad he knew about Dad. You seem to get special treatment if your dad is a minister.

At the end of May 1944, hundreds of army lorries arrive and park on the side roads around our house. American soldiers tinker with the motors, but they won't explain anything. Dad says to Mum, "There's nothing on the BBC or in the *Gloucester Citizen*, but something big is going to happen!"

Just as abruptly as they came, the soldiers move out. Endless convoys of jeeps and lorries stream down Finlay Road, the main route around Gloucester to the south coast. Jonathan and I watch them pass. As they roll by, I notice huddled inside the lorries hundreds—no, thousands—of soldiers. They're not smiling like Corporal May used to but look frightened. I run inside to ask Dad, "Can we wave like Winston Churchill?"

"Yes," he says.

Our V-for-victory salute cheers them up. Some of the soldiers wave back and throw cubes of American sugar or packs of chewing gum. The driver of one of the lorries points to us. "Here you go!" He throws something that looks like a ball. I recognize it from Corporal May's photograph.

It lands on the sloping grass in front of our house and rolls back across the sidewalk. We gasp as it bounces off the curb and out under the lorries into the center of the road. We wait for hours and hours, praying it won't get squashed. At last, the jeep at the end of the long convoy drives by, and I dash out into the road to pick it up.

I proudly take it inside as if it were a gift from the president of the United States—a fabulous American orange! Dad shows us how to peel and separate it into segments for everybody: one for Mum, one for Dad, one for Jonathan, and one for me. There are even enough for the Jacksons, who live next door.

Nothing ever tasted so sweet! I wish I could live in America.

Several days later I hear on the radio about the invasion of Normandy by Allied troops. Many of them get killed. I hope Corporal May is all right.

Dad seems inspired by the invasion. Before bedtime Saturday night, he polishes the gold pocket watch Mum gave him on their wedding day. With a glint in his eye he says to Mum, "The war will be over soon."

Now that I'm seven, Mum thinks I should go to a better school. A future minister needs a good education. She scrapes together the fee to send me to grammar school. Founded in 1666, the same year as the great fire of London, it's grandly named after Sir Thomas Rich, but we call it Tommy Rich's. Our motto is, "Garde ta foy," which means "keep your faith." This seems quite necessary in our run-down, dilapidated classrooms. The battered wooden desks bear the carved initials of generations of students. Mr. Tully, our math teacher, snorts, "This is a dustbin grammar school!" We hope to get a new building after the war, as Dad hopes to get a new chapel at Trinity.

Sometimes Mum gets up in the middle of the night trembling with chills and fever from malaria. She turns red with sweating and can't go to chapel, but she never complains. I notice two plates of false teeth. She puts them in a glass of water for safekeeping at night and is touchy if I see her doing it. She had all her teeth taken out while she was a missionary in India.

On March 4, 1945, nine months after the excitement surrounding the invasion of Normandy, Mum has another baby. Dad gets what he wanted—a girl. With tears in his eyes, he goes into the bedroom to see Mum after the delivery. He suggests calling his daughter Ruth Mary after a favorite aunt.

But Mum says, "We're not going to call her Mary. We should call her Joy because she has given you so much pleasure." They settle on Ruth Joy.

After the usual postdelivery week in bed, Mum is eager to get back to running church activities. She says her breast milk has dried up. Dad babysits on Wednesday afternoons so she can return to the women's meeting. He gives Ruth a bottle at night and rocks her to sleep. Ruth cries and vomits a lot, and it takes Dr. Green several months to find a formula she can digest.

On May 5, 1945, Germany surrenders. For the first time in weeks the sun breaks through the clouds. I run up and down the garden path waving a small Union Jack and shouting, "We won the war! We won the war!"

A warm glow spreads through me when Pete May, promoted to sergeant, comes to visit us on his way back to America.

We're still at war with Japan. Tens of thousands of Allied troops get killed fighting over islands in the Pacific. Dad says, "It's going to get worse if we have to invade the mainland." Suddenly, President Truman authorizes the use of the atomic bomb on Hiroshima and Nagasaki. On September 2, Japan surrenders. I trot up and down the garden path again with the Union Jack, waving to the Jacksons across the fence.

Strangely enough, although I don't realize it at the time, the end of the world war marks the beginning of my personal war with Mum.

# Chapter Four

## *MUM RULES OUT FARMING*

Now that we have won the war against Germany, I assume we will soon get a new school and Dad will get a new church. The Labour Party sweeps Winston Churchill out of office in July 1945, and Dad says the new prime minister, Clement Atlee, has promised a "New Jerusalem." But life doesn't get any better. We're short of everything and bread is rationed. Mum tells us to clean the dirt off our knees with a pumice stone because there is no soap. She still cuts up the newspaper into little squares for us to use as toilet paper.

On the Lord's Day she sends Jonathan and me to chapel with the Boys' Brigade at ten o'clock, the regular morning service at eleven, Sunday school at three, and the gospel service at six. We hear all the Bible stories and a lot of sermons. On Tuesday nights she marches us off to Young Warriors, where she drills us in our motto, "If Jesus Christ be God and died for me, then no sacrifice can be too great for me to make for him." She knows all about sacrifice because she was a missionary in India for seven years. Her face glows with enthusiasm. She has dedicated me to the Lord's service.

She raises money for the missionaries by distributing wooden boxes that look like the telephone at Grandpa Hadley's house. The boxes have a small round black speaker in front, a slot for coins, and a slogan in bold letters across the front that says, SEND A MESSAGE TO THE HEATHEN. When the boxes are full, Mum removes a seal at the bottom and counts the coins on the dining room table. There are a lot of pennies, some sixpences and shillings, and a few half crowns. She sends the money to the Lakher Pioneer Mission.

All week at home Mum cracks out orders like the wind snapping the wet sheets on the clothesline. "Dust the living room. Wax the floors. Polish the silver. Wash the dishes. Cut the lawn. Weed the garden. Feed the fowls. Take care of Ruth." I don't like her bossing me around.

One afternoon after Sunday school I get carried away. I swing around a post at the entrance to the chapel with two girls. Mum suddenly walks out the door. She demands, "Stop that at once."

I can't help myself. "Here's one for Mrs. Ball," I yell, and swing around again. The girls laugh. Mum scowls.

As soon as we get home she says sternly, "You were very cheeky! Go and get the hairbrush." It streaks though the air. A burning blow makes my hand crumple. I wince and brace for the next whack.

Mum seldom needs to hit Jonathan because he always does what she says. When I resist an order, her face turns white. Once, when she loses her temper, she packs such a wallop that the hairbrush breaks in half over my hand. I hope for a second she'll quit, but no such luck. She finds another brush.

She refuses to let us go to the pictures because it would be sinful, just like dancing, smoking, drinking, or gambling. Since Dad is a minister, we must set an example. When I go secretly to see a Roy Rogers movie with some school friends, I suddenly get in a sweat. What if the Lord returns and finds me at the pictures? I feel so scared, I get up and run out in the middle.

Mum sends me to evening classes to prepare for the scripture exam. This involves memorizing verses and Bible stories. Sunday schools throughout Gloucester compete for a silver shield. Since Trinity is a fairly new school, we've never won the trophy. I want to do my best for Trinity and for Mum.

Long after the exam, as I play cricket on the Calton Road field with the Boys' Brigade, Mum rattles toward us over the bumpy grass on her bicycle. She talks and smiles with our captain, but pedals off into the growing darkness without speaking to me.

Our captain says, "Do you know why your mother came?"

"No."

"You were first in your age group in the scripture exam. Trinity has won the shield!"

I know Mum must be pleased although I'm disappointed she didn't tell me herself. She never hugs me or praises anything I do. But Dad says, "The results will be announced at a big meeting at city hall. I want you to receive the shield for Trinity."

I listen carefully to Dad when he preaches about sin and damnation. It's pretty scary! At the end of the sermon he invites those who want to be saved from the fires of hell to come forward. The congregation hums with electricity as we wait for someone to move. I know I'm a sinner in need of forgiveness, but I sit tight and uncomfortable. I don't want to go forward in front of all these people.

Mum corners me in the front hall to tell me breathlessly that Jonathan has given his heart to the Lord. What a shock! He never mentioned it to me. This could be a problem because I can sense Mum wants me to be converted too. But her sudden enthusiasm makes me suspicious, and I feel trapped just like in the gas mask.

I need to do something because I'm afraid of going to hell. After thinking it over for a long time, I kneel alone by my bed and say, "Lord, I believe you died on the cross to forgive my sins. Please come into my heart." I don't see a light from heaven like Dad says he did as a young man, yet in the quiet I know God has forgiven me.

At Boys' Brigade chapel, Dad teaches us how to pray. We bow our heads and close our eyes. He tells us to put our hands over our faces and try to shut all worldly thoughts out of our minds. It works! In the privacy of my praying hands with my breath warm on my face, I find it easy to talk to God.

While Dad preaches fire and brimstone from the pulpit, he is meek and mild around the house. Every morning he feeds the fowls, shines our shoes, and takes Mum a cup of tea in bed, before he sticks his head around our bedroom door and says in a warm, kind voice, "Time for breakfast!" When Jonathan and I cycle off to school, he waves good-bye.

Jonathan goes to the King's School, founded for the choirboys at Gloucester Cathedral. Sometimes we get separated in the thick early morning fog and he calls out, "Dave, where are you?" He likes us to be together, and I know I can always count on him.

I hear on the BBC that the government has decided to pull out of India. I ask Mum, "What will happen to the Lakher Pioneer Mission?"

She replies, "We must pray for them. They need all the help they can get." She continues to urge her followers to use the collection boxes to SEND A MESSAGE TO THE HEATHEN.

Mum takes full advantage of having Dad around the house. On Monday mornings he helps her wash the laundry. We have a large metal boiler that heats the water and fills the kitchen with steam. In go all the dirty clothes. Dad stirs them with a big stick. When the water turns soapy brown, he runs the clothes through the mangle and hangs them to dry on the line outside. Years later I learn that several gardens down, Sylvia Lawrence (who played tennis with Dad before he met Mum) thinks it rather odd to see a man hanging the washing.

Mum doesn't enjoy cooking. Rice pudding usually features in Sunday dinner because that was what she had in India. She puts it in the oven just before we leave for chapel. If Dad preaches a long sermon, the rice burns and looks like little brown bullets. Jonathan always cleans his plate without any argument. When I object, Mum says, "You'll sit there until you eat it. Just think of all those starving orphans in India."

While crushing any rebellion at home, Mum also distances herself from her own family. I first notice this strange silence when Grandpa Hadley's wealthy sister, Aunt Mona, gives her a portrait of one of her Hadley ancestors, a little boy with red-brown hair. Dad says, "Aunt Mona wanted Mum to become her companion and secretary after finishing school. She has named her in her will." Mum hangs the painting on the wall behind her threadbare seat in the living room, but she never explains how she is related to the boy. Holding a top hat in one hand and a hoop in the other, the poor fellow standing behind her chair seems more like a ghost.

In fact, as Mum becomes more zealous, her entire family might just as well be ghosts. Mum dismisses them all with, "They're too worldly." We seldom visit Granny Hadley at The Lawn. We never see Mum's youngest sister who lives on the Gloucester-Sharpness barge canal, in a bungalow that Granny inherited from someone named Uncle Bert. I can't imagine why Uncle Bert gave Granny the bungalow. Mum never talks about it.

I don't have any reason to think about Mum's relations until the headmaster of Tommy Rich's decides the school should have a crew that can practice on the canal. He says the cox should be the smallest boy in the school who can swim. This happens to be me. When I enter the Gloucester Rowing Club for the first time, I notice on the wall a photograph of my grandpa, Victor Hadley. As soon as I get home, I demand an explanation. Mum says, "He was president of the club."

"What else did he do that I don't know about?"

"He was a merchant at the corn exchange. During the war he was Food Controller overseeing all the grain going through Gloucester." Although she keeps her voice even, I sense she is proud of him. But I also sense she holds something back.

The news on the BBC sounds grim. Prime Minister Clement Atlee announces a new round of belt-tightening. Food, clothing, and petrol are still strictly rationed. Dad says, "The country is bankrupt. We owe the United States three thousand million pounds."

I ask, "When will we get a new school and a new church?"

He replies, "As long as we are broke and our cities are full of bomb sites heaped with rubble there won't be money for schools and churches. We need to produce goods for export."

Dad wants a car. He claims ministers get priority, but he seems stuck on the waiting list.

Occasionally, he borrows Granny Hadley's car and drives us to Sunny Bank in the Cotswolds, where his father raises a few beef cattle and fowls, keeps a cow for milking, and cuts his wheat by hand with a scythe. Dad's mother died when he was eleven, and after many years his father has married a cheerful lady we call Auntie Gracie. She and Grandfather live simply, but her favorite exclamation is, "What a blessing!"

One unforgettable Saturday at Sunny Bank we notice a rabbit sitting in the middle of a field nibbling the lush grass. Dad has a brilliant idea. He whispers, "Stay perfectly still. I'll come around from the other side." He advances stealthily along the hedge and stuns his quarry with a heavy stick. When we get home, he skins the rabbit and puts it in a pot to cook with onions, carrots, and peas from our garden. Everyone loves rabbit stew. We haven't had meat for weeks.

We have a tradition of gathering at Sunny Bank with Dad's family just once a year on Boxing Day, the day after Christmas. As we drive through Cheltenham, Dad insists on stopping to watch the hunt meet in front of the Queens Hotel. Children on ponies circle the scarlet-coated master to deliver their capping fees for the privilege of hunting that day. Gentlemen in black jackets, white stocks, and gleaming leather boots clatter back and forth with great importance. The hounds swirl around the huntsman. Suddenly, they're off.

Dad says, "When I was a boy, I opened a gate for the Prince of Wales, who was out with the Berkeley Hunt. One of the people with him gave me a shilling."

I know I don't belong to this splendid gentleman's world, but I wish I did.

At Sunny Bank, Jonathan and I escape Mum's control for secret pranks with our cousins. Steam billows from the kitchen where Auntie Gracie conjures up beetroots, potatoes, carrots, peas, turkey, and Christmas pudding, and exclaims, "What a blessing!" The linoleum runs with condensation. We take off our shoes and skate in our socks down the hallway, screaming with laughter until it's time to squash into the small dining room. We gasp with excitement when Grandfather, who is a teetotaler, pours brandy over the Christmas pudding and lights it with a match. We plead for large portions, knowing the pudding is stuffed with silver thruppenny bits. Then, full of high spirits, we head for the bluebell wood to cut holly and mistletoe for home.

The only other time Mum doesn't tell me what to do occurs when we visit Dad's sister, Auntie Vera, and Uncle Gerald at Kington Mead Farm, near Thornbury. We delight in the company of their children Roger and Carol, but most of all we admire their daredevil son John. The moment we arrive, Jonathan and I pile out of the car and yell, "Where's John?"

Auntie Vera often replies, "I just sent him out to mark the lines of the tennis court." But he's gone. Our cousin seems to disappear just before we get there. We find him bird nesting or shooting magpies with his air rifle or once kissing a girl behind the summer house. We follow him like the Pied Piper through the rich smell of cow manure in the yard, where the cattle wait for milking, to the world of freedom and adventure beyond the gate.

*David in front and Jonathan on a farm horse at Kington Mead Farm in 1943.*

Despite rationing, lunch on the farm often includes ham from Uncle Gerald's pigs or cheese made with milk from his cows. Sometimes Auntie picks gooseberries and tells me, "I'm going to cook your favorite pudding—Oldbury tarts." At bedtime she always says, "The end of another happy day!" She gives me a candle to light my way down the cold flagstone hall and up the stairs to my bedroom. It feels romantic that the farmhouse has no electricity.

One day Auntie calls me to the window. "Look, David!" I feel a thrill as we watch the Berkeley hunt galloping across home field.

During harvest Dad helps Uncle Gerald pile sheaves of wheat onto the hay wagon in Gully field near Thornbury Castle. Jonathan and I perch on top of the sheaves while the horses clip-clop the heavy load back to the barn. We're level with the neighbor Mr. Thurston, who stands on a ladder trimming his topiaries. These large yew trees, cut in the shape of a bride and a groom, look dressed up to celebrate our royal progress. Uncle Gerald and Dad stop to talk. I pluck mulberries from a tree leaning over the road.

I am still blissfully unaware of Mum's plan for my life, but back in the farmhouse she says, "I want you and Jonathan to sing a trio with me at Oldbury Chapel."

I think of her quavering singing voice and protest, "No, I'd be embarrassed."

She insists, "You should do it to please the Lord."

When I still refuse, she leaves me to think it over. She's always talking about me pleasing the Lord. It twists in my mind. Part of me wants to obey her, but I can't.

Usually, I steer clear of Uncle Gerald, a no-nonsense person, on fire to win souls for the Lord. One evening after dinner, while we sit round the table in the front room of the farmhouse in the soft light of the kerosene lamp, he asks, "David, how would you like to preach at Oldbury Chapel?" I know I'm rather young at eleven years of age, but I like the idea. I've listened to hundreds of Dad's sermons and I know what to say. It doesn't occur to me until years later that Mum must have enlisted Uncle Gerald in her campaign to march me into the ministry.

I decide to talk about a passage in the sixth chapter of Ephesians about putting on the whole armor of God and spend hours preparing my message. I love the details about the pieces of armor: "the shield of faith," "the helmet of salvation," and "the sword of the Spirit." When Dad reads over what I have prepared, he says, "That's pretty good!" Mum nods her head, but she lets Dad do the talking.

I cycle the twenty-three miles to Thornbury with a friend, but to my dismay Auntie Vera, John, and Carol are away on holiday. On Sunday, I walk boldly into the pulpit to deliver my sermon. The small congregation of adults and children from the village of Oldbury show no objection to an eleven-year-old preacher. In fact, they watch fascinated as my friend illustrates my message using a flannel-graph board with cutouts of different pieces of armor.

My accomplishment deepens my bond with Kington Mead Farm. A general delight in this magical place colors my thoughts about what to do when I grow up. What about farming? I know Uncle Gerald has to fetch the cows for milking in the pouring rain. In the winter he works outside in the muck and freezing cold. Would I be willing to do that?

I mull it over for a long time and finally I decide. Yes, I want to be a farmer.

At teatime, when I tell my parents about my decision, Mum retorts angrily, "No, David, I don't think that's a good idea."

Stunned, I look across at her. Why is she against my being a farmer?

# Chapter Five

## *Mum Schemes*

After Mum eliminates farming as a possible career, I forget about it until my class at Tommy Rich's is interrupted by a visit from the headmaster. He summons us to the master's desk one at a time to assign us to different academic programs.

"Ball, what are your plans?"

I've no idea. Apart from wanting to be a farmer, I've never thought about any particular calling. On the spur of the moment I reply, "I'd like to be a minister like my father."

"Good!" exclaims the headmaster. "I'll assign you to the humanities."

At home, on hearing the news, Mum is ecstatic, almost singing with delight. "Well done! Just what I expected. When you were born I dedicated you to the Lord's service."

I bask in her approval. I've never seen her like this before. By accident, I must have done the right thing! As I lie in my bedroom above the living room, I hear the triumphant murmur of her voice as she makes plans with Dad.

The next Sunday, Jonathan and I take our usual position, third row from the front, for the morning service. One of the deacons, who is also my Sunday school teacher, approaches, looking serious. He says, "I need to ask you several questions. Do you believe that Jesus Christ died on the cross to forgive your sins and rose again from the dead?"

"Yes."

"Have you accepted the Lord Jesus Christ as your own personal Savior?"

"Yes."

"Would you like to be baptized and join the church?"

"I would."

Now he smiles. "Good! There will be several young people from Trinity, including your cousin Roger Staley."

I like the idea of becoming a member of Dad's church. It seems like moving up to a higher form at school, only more important. Not only that, after sitting empty-handed all my life, now I'll be able to take communion. It will be an outward sign of how I feel inside.

Since our temporary chapel building at Trinity has no tank of water, Dad conducts the service downtown at Brunswick Road Baptist Church, where Mum was baptized when she was fourteen years old. She stands with the girls at the side of the baptistry, but as I walk forward in my white shirt and cricket trousers, I notice her beaming in my direction. Dad plunges me backward below the surface of the water. I find my feet and step out purposefully to dry off like a new man.

Dad himself seems like a new man in June when he sails off for six weeks to attend the World Baptist Convention in Cleveland, Ohio. He says, "There aren't many Baptists in England, but there are a lot of them in America."

His sister, Auntie Doris, teases Mum, "How could you let him be away for so long?"

Mum replies sternly, "He's on the Lord's business!" She keeps everybody organized at the chapel.

We all look forward to his return. On the big day I ask Mum, "Can we fly the Union Jack over the gate?"

"Yes, you may, and when you've done that go and cut the front lawn."

At last Dad walks up the driveway under the flag. He mutters, "You shouldn't have made such a fuss." But when we sit down for tea he creates a stir himself with a startling announcement. "Irene, I've received an invitation to a Baptist church in Texas."

"Wow!" I can't help interrupting. "Oh please, let's go to America!"

Mum quickly squelches the idea. "The Lord needs us here at Trinity."

Later I ask Dad why she doesn't want to go. "She wants to stay near her family," he replies. How strange when we hardly ever see them.

Mum makes all the important decisions. She never acknowledges any personal consideration. She pronounces edicts as if she received the word from God. In fact, when I learn in school about the divine right of kings, it sounds just like Mum. She seems to think her will and God's are the same.

Dad's expedition to America encourages me to seek permission to go to France with the Bristol-Bordeaux exchange program sponsored by local schools. I use my best argument with Mum. "It will help me find out what it's like living in another country."

"That's true," she replies. "You might be a missionary one day!"

At age fourteen I spend a month with a family in Libourne and attend school with their son, Pierre. We visit a vineyard owned by Pierre's relatives. They offer red or white wine instead of milk. This puts me on the spot. Mum signed a pledge with the Women's Christian Temperance Union that I would not touch strong drink while under her care. However, I don't want to offend. After a few meals, I get used to the wine. Funny! It's not as bad as I thought.

When I return to Gloucester, I tell Mum, "I drank wine. I had no choice." She glares at me but doesn't say anything.

Although I never question Mum's partnership with Dad at Trinity, I puzzle about their relationship at home. Ruth, age six, still sleeps on a small cot next to my parents' double bed. I ask Mum, "When is Ruth going to move into the spare bedroom?"

"She's not going to move. We need it for visitors," she replies.

I wonder why Mum doesn't want to sleep alone in the bedroom with Dad. She never kisses him, but I bet he'd like it if she did.

Mum and Dad never discuss sex. What little I know, I learn from boys at school. When we start biology with Mr. Sinkinson, who uses an old tie to hold up his trousers, we don't realize he will cover an important part of our education. Attention picks up instantly when he discusses "the reproductive system male" and "the reproductive system female."

The only girls I know come to chapel. I like Janet, who is pretty and talks and laughs with me when the Young Warriors play rounders. On the train back from Young Warrior camp at Weymouth, she encourages me to place my arms around her as we stand looking out the window. A few weeks later, I see her walking hand in hand with another boy. How could she do that? I thought she liked me. The sting lingers for days.

In September 1951, our form master talks about a coming national election. He seems to think after six years of austerity people want a change. He asks, "If you could vote in the election, which party would you choose?"

I've never considered this before. Mum votes Conservative. Her father was a member of the Gloucester Conservative Club. Dad, who admires Lloyd George as a champion of nonconformists, votes Liberal. Since I feel closer to Dad, I raise my hand for the Liberals.

When the national election is held in October, the Conservatives win and Winston Churchill returns as prime minister. To the great joy of everyone in the family he ends rationing.

Dad finally gets a new car called a Morris Minor. The word *minor* seems appropriate for such a small car, but it's amazing how many people we can pack into it.

Excitement picks up at school in February 1952 when the bell rings unexpectedly in the afternoon summoning us to the main hall. The boys line up, form by form, just as we do for prayers at the beginning of the day. I ask my friend, Graham Ring, "Why are we here?"

"Don't know," he replies. "Must be terribly important!"

The headmaster strides in wearing his black gown, stands at the rostrum in front of the students, and proclaims in a loud dramatic voice, "The king is dead. Long live the queen!"

Shock and sadness settle over the school, and in that moment I remember how the king refused to leave Buckingham Palace after it was bombed. But we recover quickly as the pianist strikes up the national anthem on the piano—the same old tune but one different word! Three hundred of us sing with great emotion, "God Save the Queen."

The next day, another friend, John Evans, and I rush to the end of Eastgate Street, where the old gate of the walled city used to stand. We want to see the royal herald, attired with knee breeches, a red jacket, and a cocked hat, ring a handbell and proclaim our new monarch. There are pictures in the newspaper of Elizabeth's return to London from Kenya, where she was on vacation. Winston Churchill stands at attention to greet her as she steps down from her plane.

Small for my age, I don't like being called "Tichy Ball" by my classmates. Dad rubs it in by saying I am the brains and Jonathan, who is taller and better at sports, is the brawn. When my history teacher starts calling me Tichy Ball, I know I must do something about it.

I try to eat more, but school lunches composed of waterlogged cabbage and gristle disguised with gravy prove hopeless. I also copy the rugby players, who drink a lot of milk during the morning break. First thing every day I power through push-ups in my bedroom. At rugby practice on Wednesday afternoons, I hustle as scrum half.

In rugby, unlike American football, there are fifteen players on each team and forward passes are not allowed. We must pass the ball sideways or backwards. The game takes a lot of stamina because it is continuous and there is no substitution. We get three points for a try, which means grounding the ball behind your opponents' goal line, and two more for a conversion. My job is to pass the ball to the players in the backfield as quickly as possible after it is heeled by the forwards in the scrum. If I don't move fast enough, I risk getting smashed by the other team.

By the time the next rugby season comes around, I have shot up to five foot eleven inches, almost as tall as Dad. After seeing me speed through a house game, the head coach tells me to practice with the "first thirty," which provides the players for the top rugby teams. Several weeks later the scrum half for the second fifteen leaves school and I take his place. To my astonishment and great joy, I scoop up a loose ball and dash to score a try. A month later I move up to the first fifteen. I listen with satisfaction as the headmaster announces my name in the school team for the next game. Nobody calls me Tichy Ball anymore.

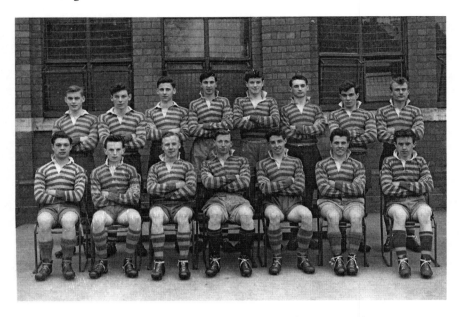

*Sir Thomas Rich's School 1st XV Rugby Team with
David in front row second from left, 1954*

The city of Gloucester has one of the best rugby teams in the country. After the thrill of playing scrum half for the school, I shower and join a group of boys heading for Kingsholm, the city rugby grounds. For one shilling we occupy concrete stands and yell our heads off. "Go Gloucester!" After the game, we go to the pictures. I don't run out in the middle of the film now, but of course I don't tell Mum I've been.

Directly across the field from the concrete stands at Kingsholm, an enclosed area rises where spectators pay two shillings and sixpence for a seat. As I cheer for Gloucester, I see my uncle Cyril Dancey, Auntie Joyce's husband, a prominent architect and chief magistrate, sitting in one of the expensive spots. I remember him telling me he knew Mum as a girl when she was the tennis champion and a "flapper." He said, "I liked her auburn hair and the way she danced." She doesn't sound anything like the Mum I know.

I haven't spoken to Uncle Cyril in ages because we live in a different social world. I think the Danceys regard us as their poor relatives. Once a year when Auntie Joyce buys a new dress, she gives an old one to Mum. Mum is always grateful.

The Danceys belong to the Church of England just as Mum did as a child. When she was a teenager, she switched to Brunswick Road Baptist. She never explains why. Since Baptists don't belong to the state church, we are dismissed as nonconformists, which seems to make us a little lower on the social scale.

Most of the time I don't mind being called a nonconformist. On the first Sunday of every month, I march through the run-down houses in the White City with the Trinity Boys' Brigade band. When we parade downtown with the army and Sea Cadets to give thanks for the end of the fighting in Korea, I swing my tenor drumsticks high in the air. Jonathan carries the flag. Dad marches with the officers. The great west doors of the cathedral that are usually bolted shut spring open, and we file straight into the nave with the other Gloucester boys.

However, even though I plan to be a minister, I resent Mum exposing me to ridicule. On Sunday evenings in the summer she insists that I participate in "open-air meetings." This involves Dad's holding a service on a street corner and broadcasting the message with a loudspeaker. He urges the sinners in the White City, some of whom are my classmates at school, to confess their sins and come to the Lord.

One Sunday I ask Dad, "Would you mind if Jonathan and I don't come?"

"Well … all right," he agrees reluctantly.

I make the mistake of telling Mum that Dad has let us off the hook. "Don't talk nonsense," she snaps. "Of course you're going!"

She has the same stern attitude when I ask about joining a tennis club. Granny Hadley has sold the bottom of the garden at The Lawn. This includes the tennis court Grandpa built for his children. With Graham Ring I want to join the tennis club that uses it. Mum forbids me.

I recollect once when I was a little boy Mum had prevented me from getting the tennis racquets out of the summer house. For some reason it made her upset, but I don't see what that's got to do with now.

"You played there when you were young," I plead. "What's wrong with the tennis club?"

"They're not Christians," she retorts in a tone that brooks no further discussion. It's so unfair. Mum puts a damper on everything!

Without mentioning it at home, I ask the headmaster at Tommy Rich's for permission to drop Latin. He moves me out of the fast-track program for students going to university. Big mistake! I land in a different class from the boys I admire, like Graham Ring. Toward the end of the school year I ask to return to fast track. The headmaster approves, but insists, "You should take Greek. You'll need it for the ministry." I would agree to anything to get back with my friends. He adds, "You must also catch up on all the work you've missed during the year!"

My history teacher, Angus Johnson, tells us about playing rugby for his college, Christ Church, at Oxford. He was picked to play for the Greyhounds, which might have led to playing for Oxford, but a great snowstorm in the winter of 1947 prevented any rugby that year. He takes us to watch Oxford play Cambridge before a huge crowd at Twickenham.

One morning, instead of teaching history, Angus Johnson describes studying under the personal supervision of a tutor. At Christ Church he met with his tutor once a week and the tutor assigned books to read and papers to write. His research required study in the Bodleian Library, which is so big it tunnels under the main street. He raves about a ball at the end of term that lasted until sunrise where he and his girlfriend danced barefoot in the fountain in the middle of the quad.

That evening I tell my parents, "I want to go to Oxford!"

Mum kills the idea fast. "It is too worldly."

When I go to bed, I hear the murmur of her voice giving instructions to Dad in the living room below. The next day Dad corners me after supper. He says, "You need to think about preparing for the ministry. You can choose between two good colleges—London Bible College and Moody Bible Institute."

The decision doesn't take long. I forget about Oxford. I know that London Bible College has a rugby team. But Moody Bible Institute has something better—America! Compared with postwar England, the streets in America must be paved with gold. What's more, I find a seductive detail in the Moody catalogue. It says fifty percent of the students marry other Moody students. I tell Jonathan, "I'm going to be part of that fifty percent!" Full of excitement, I read my Bible every night and start a diary about my spiritual journey.

In January, soon after Moody accepts my application, I hear Dad conferring with Mum. "The time is right. Jonathan will be leaving King's School. Ruth is only eight. It would be easy for her to make the change."

For the first time, she doesn't stamp on the idea of emigration. "Let's pray about it."

Every evening before they go to bed they kneel down by their chairs in the living room to ask God to guide them. But, of course, I don't know about their prayers. I can't wait to escape from Mum's control.

As leader of the local Youth for Christ meetings, Dad organizes support for an evangelistic campaign by the Reverend Billy Graham at Harringay Stadium in London. He invites the other Gloucester nonconformist ministers to meet with the Billy Graham team for planning and prayer. They sponsor a weekly broadcast from the campaign to Brunswick Road Baptist Church. I have never seen so many young people in church.

The sponsors also arrange for buses to take us to Harringay and the final rally at Wembley Stadium attended by one hundred thousand people.

Amazed by the huge crowds, I ask Dad, "Is this a revival?"

"I hope so," he replies. "It happened before with John Wesley and Dwight Moody."

I hope so too. It would vindicate Dad's ministry. Besides, it would be particularly grand with Billy Graham's being an American.

One night early in 1954, when Mum and Dad finish praying, Mum announces a startling change of mind. "Well that's it! I feel it's God's will we go to America!"

Astounded though pleased, Dad wonders if she believes it's God's will because there will be more opportunity for her children. He readily agrees to her condition that they live in a town, not the country. Then she gets to the heart of the matter! "We'll be able to help David prepare for the ministry."

I'm not going to be allowed out there on my own.

# Chapter Six

## *MY FIRST YEAR IN AMERICA*

When Mum decides to go to America, the air fizzes out of my dream of independence. She's moving the whole family to keep an eye on me. I don't mind about Dad, but I don't want Mum telling me what to do.

At Trinity, Dad preaches about Moses leaving Egypt for the Promised Land. He says, "I too feel called to a new place and a new service." He helps the congregation find a replacement. After twenty-two good years at Trinity, he confronts an uncertain future in setting off with his wife and children without a job. He looks thin and concerned. Postwar currency restrictions mean he can take only fifty pounds from his savings.

Mum, on the other hand, seems supremely confident. She has forgotten her previous reluctance to go to America. In a farewell letter in the chapel bulletin, she admonishes, "I know you would not have us be disobedient to the prompting of his Holy Spirit." For her, it's just like going to India as a missionary. She doesn't fuss about leaving Granny Hadley or her sisters, but a few weeks before we sail, she insists on driving all the way to Bristol to say good-bye to Aunt Mona.

While Mum and Dad are moving out of the house, Jonathan and I stay nearby on Finlay Road with George and Sylvia Lawrence. They used to attend Trinity, but left to help with another mission church founded by Dad in Lower Tuffley. I don't know that Dad once admired Sylvia. She seems very strict.

Dad's sisters, Auntie Vera and Auntie Doris, and their husbands take us to Southampton. As I rush eagerly up the gangway onto the *SS United States*, it doesn't occur to me to look back and wave good-bye. America, a promised land flowing with milk and honey, beckons.

The sleek ocean liner has just won the blue ribbon for the fastest crossing of the Atlantic in three and a half days. I have never seen anything so magnificent with deck above deck like a huge many-layered wedding cake. The first-class passengers even have a swimming pool. Of course we travel third class. Jonathan and I share a cabin with two older men from the crew in the bowels of the ship.

Eager for adventure, we explore the mysterious stairs and passageways and find an untended turnstile. By crawling under the horizontal bar we can reach the forbidden pleasures of first class. We dash back to our cabin for our bathing costumes. My heart thumps when we slide under the turnstile and sneak into one of the dressing rooms alongside the swimming pool. In the privacy of the changing area, we laugh hysterically at our daring and forget the need for caution until an attendant glares at us with suspicion. Careful not to attract any more attention, we revel in the water sloshing from side to side while the *SS United States* speeds toward America.

As we approach New York, a friendly American couple who challenged us to Ping-Pong urge us to watch for something important. The husband says mysteriously, "You'll have to be on deck by six o'clock." We don't have a clue what to expect, but set our alarm for just before six.

We arrive on deck at daybreak. A haze over the water promises a hot day. As the tugboat pulls us into the harbor, Jonathan shouts, "Dave, look!" Upright in the fog, a figure with a raised arm greets us. We hang over the rail for our first experience of America—the Statue of Liberty growing larger and larger.

So it is on July 18, 1954, our family stands on the dock at Thirty-Third Street in New York, with three trunks and five suitcases containing all our worldly possessions. Everything else was sold with our home on Finlay Road or given away. In my pocket I have two quarters that Dad gave me for my foreign coin collection.

As we wait for our wartime friend Sergeant May, Jonathan yells, "Wow, look at those huge cars!" Bright yellow taxis, twice as large as

Dad's tiny Morris Minor, whiz along an elevated highway. I watch eagerly for Pete May's car, which must be grand. But he arrives on foot.

"Where's your car?" I ask.

He chuckles. "I was worried about city traffic, so I left it in a parking lot in New Jersey."

We deposit our luggage at the Thomas Cook travel office, while Pete May takes us to see Times Square and Broadway. He escorts us up three different elevators to the top of the Empire State Building. It sways in the wind, and I want to get back to the ground as soon as possible. Unlike England where it seldom gets over seventy, the temperature soars to a shocking one hundred degrees. We sit under shade trees in Bryant Park in the back of the New York Public Library to eat sandwiches and escape from the sidewalk crowds. I can hardly believe we're in America.

Dad must feel good too. He asks Pete May, "What do you think of President Eisenhower?"

Our hero grins. "Ike's still the same guy with a big smile who got us together for the Normandy landing."

As we head upstate, I marvel at the paradise of my dreams. Grand Central Station is a shining palace compared with Gloucester's two grimy old railway stations. The high-speed diesel-powered Empire State Express brilliantly surpasses the coal-fired, smoke-puffing steam engines we have left behind. In Buffalo we are welcomed by Dad's roommate at Moody, Charlie Gould, who takes us to his home in a town actually called Eden. Bursting with excitement, Jonathan and I discover he has three good-looking daughters who like to be teased.

But one thing hasn't changed. On Sunday we attend the regular morning service and the young people's meeting at an evangelical church. After lunch Mum says, "David, you should come to the gospel service tonight."

For the first time in my life, in a flash of independence that takes both of us by surprise, I reply, "I'm not going."

"What are you talking about?"

"I'm not going."

She raises her voice. "You're not pleasing the Lord!"

Jonathan goes along, but I dig in. While I was growing up she sent me to church four times every Sunday and now I think twice is enough.

When I refuse again the following Sunday evening, Mum screams, "You're training to be a minister. The Lord expects you to be in church!"

I shout back at the top of my lungs, "I've already been to church." However, after they leave, I feel a twinge of guilt.

When the family takes me to the train for Chicago, Jonathan cries. We've never been separated before. I'm touched, but I can't wait to get to Moody.

I arrive at Union Station in Chicago with my dilapidated suitcase, which needs to be held together by one of Dad's belts ever since the lock broke. The suitcase contains a thick concordance and several translations of the Bible as well as my clothes. As I lug my heavy load up LaSalle Street, some men in a car try to pick me up. I quickly cross to the other side of the road and stay on the alert until I reach Moody.

Moody covers an entire inner-city block at 820 North LaSalle Street, and students come here to prepare for the evangelical ministry or the mission field. The program has a familiar feel. My education and training at home prepared me well for the Pastors' Course. I excel in English, French, and Greek. I already know the Bible inside out. In Practical Preaching, I fervently emulate Billy Graham with dramatic gestures, urging my startled speechless classmates to repent.

Despite my rebellion at the Goulds's, I want to be a good minister. Confident of my calling and free of Mum's command, I get up at six each morning to kneel in the dorm with three other men to read the Bible and pray. With boundless energy, I teach Sunday school in a rough part of the inner city and venture into run-down apartment buildings to invite children to come to the storefront church where Moody students hold services. What's more, I volunteer to witness on street corners, despite my previous aversion to "open-air meetings" in the White City in Gloucester. Strangely enough, when Mum comes to visit, I enjoy showing her around.

I submit a poem about my spiritual journey to the student newspaper and the editor offers me space for a new poem every two weeks. The soul-searching act of writing helps me to think through what I believe.

In issue after issue I write about the wonder of God's love and his presence in my life. Nobody can argue about it. I talk to him every day. I even try some hymns, which later are published in a hymnbook called *Great Hymns of the Faith*.

Some of the students call me "limey" and tease me about my Gloucestershire accent. This hits a nerve, so I ask, "How would you say it?" I listen carefully to their pronunciation, repeating it several times. I don't want to be different and don't like teasing in America any more than I liked Tichy Ball at Tommy Rich's.

While I settle down at Moody, Dad is invited to pastor Hartland Baptist Church, the only place of worship in the small village of Johnson Creek in western New York. Mum forgets her insistence on living in a town. Farmers with cherry and peach orchards fill the parsonage refrigerator with food and donate secondhand furniture. Dad writes that his salary of $3,200 a year is more than what he was paid at Trinity.

There is no charge for tuition or room and board at Moody, but to earn money to pay for my books, toilet articles, and bus fare to church, I work as a busboy at the Women's Athletic Club on Michigan Avenue. The money enables me to replace my broken English suitcase with a cheap model from Montgomery Ward.

Sometimes when I head for work, the gale-force wind off the lake forces me to lean forward and grab onto the ropes installed at the edge of the sidewalk. In December a snowstorm dumps four feet of snow on the city. The streetcar on Clark Avenue, which has a snowplow fixed in front to clear the way, comes to a standstill. We never had weather like this in England.

A few days before Christmas vacation, I realize I don't have any money. For the first time since I arrived in Chicago, I want to be with my family. I decide to hitchhike six hundred miles in a massive snowstorm with a sign that says, "Buffalo or Bust." A fellow student gives me a ride to Route 20 just outside of Cleveland. I stand in the slush on the side of the road with my sign and my Montgomery Ward suitcase, thumbing for a ride.

Eventually, the driver of a large tractor trailer slows down to read my sign and says, "Hop in, I'm going to Buffalo." He barrels along at sixty miles an hour through the night and drops me off on Main Street in the dark.

*David, his father and mother, Jonathan and Ruth at the parsonage at Johnson Creek, New York, in 1958.*

After hearing my story, the next person to pick me up says, "I'm the son of the Methodist minister in the next village. I'll take you to Johnson Creek." I arrive early in the morning to discover three feet of snow blown against the parsonage. I try the door, but find it locked with Mum and Dad asleep behind storm windows. Freezing in my skimpy jacket, I go over to the church and ring the bell. It tolls my message loud and clear across the sleeping village.

Dad comes out to investigate. "Well, well! It's a young man from Moody. I'll make you a cup of tea and an English breakfast." Soon I can hear the frying pan sizzling with bacon, eggs, fried tomatoes, and fried bread.

Mum beams as she introduces me to the congregation at the church door on Sunday. She announces proudly, "This is David, who's training to be a minister."

The arctic wind blows down across Canada, picks up moisture over Lake Ontario, and dumps more snow on Johnson Creek. The snowplow pushes it to the side of the road, where it piles up seven feet high so that the road looks like a tunnel through a white mountain. Dad finds a job for me at the local grocery store. I wear pajamas under my regular clothes to keep warm while I load the grocery truck. I also wear earmuffs, which we don't have in England, but my ears still tingle and turn red.

After Mum and Dad go to bed, Jonathan, Ruth, and I secretly decorate the bare Christmas tree with a package of tinsel I purchased with my earnings at the grocery store. On Christmas Day, Dad tunes in to a Canadian radio station to listen to the queen's broadcast. He reminds me about the family gathering at Sunny Bank on Boxing Day. I imagine my cousin John up to mischief, making them all laugh.

As I look around I feel proud of our new home. The local congregation has not only provided a used refrigerator, but also a secondhand television set, luxuries that we could not afford in England. At night Dad relaxes to read his Bible in a newfangled recliner covered with well-worn brown plastic. Mum usually settles in a wooden armchair to work on her knitting underneath the oil portrait given to her by Aunt Mona. Jonathan whispers, "Sometimes she watches TV."

To my astonishment I suddenly notice sitting on top of the TV one of Mum's telephone collection boxes with the familiar admonition, SEND A MESSAGE TO THE HEATHEN. I ask, "Are you using those boxes to raise money in Johnson Creek?"

"I've tried," she declares. "But they don't seem to work very well here.'"

She still suffers from bouts of malaria, but she resumes the informal role of associate pastor she had at Trinity and runs the Sunday school, the junior choir, the young people's meeting, and anything else that needs organizing. Furthermore she wants to visit church folks in their homes, just as she did in the White City in Gloucester, although it's too far down country roads in this mission field of farmers for her to bicycle.

Before long she insists that Dad teach her to drive the car. She has trouble with the driving test and repeats it several times until she finally gets her license. Jonathan and I laugh at her persistence, but we're not at all surprised. Whenever we ride with her in the car we hang onto our seats, because she grinds the gears and drives way over the speed limit.

Mum has been looking after an antique gold watch that an old lady at Trinity left to Ruth. Ruth loves the intricate design. When she has not seen it for a while, she asks, "Where is the watch that Mrs. Wall left me?"

Mum replies firmly and without apology, "I sold it and gave the money to the Lakher Pioneer Mission. You don't need a watch like that." Ruth goes to her bedroom and sobs.

One day Mum gets a letter from her sister Joyce. "Aunt Mona has cut you out of her will. She's sure you would give everything to the missionaries." Although Aunt Mona is probably right, our missionary mother must be hurt. She says nothing.

That summer, with encouragement from a lady in the congregation, she goes to a beauty parlor to get her first perm. All my life she has worn her hair in a simple, plain manner, pulled straight to the sides, rolled up, and pinned. The change is dramatic. Dad, secretly delighted, feels too shy to say it looks attractive. He teases, "Look at your mother with her fancy new hairstyle." Jonathan and I laugh. Mum rushes out of the room with tears in her eyes. Since she seldom shows her feelings, none of us knows what to do.

Was she hoping to recapture something of the popular "flapper" who played tennis and was the belle of dancing lessons? Is there part of her that regrets the severity she has embraced ever since? And what about Aunt Mona cutting her out of her will? We can only guess, because she never discusses her emotions.

Dad digs a huge vegetable garden at the side of the parsonage. With dismay he shows me the plants wilting in the oppressive summer heat. At forty-eight he looks tired and washed out. He says, "I doubt that I'll live to the biblical promise of three score years and ten. But your mother will. She's strong!"

I must have inherited her stamina because in July and August, I work for the Harrison Radiator Division of General Motors in Lockport, New York, on an assembly line called "the whip." I grab the radiator cooling fan off the line and add several small parts with a projection welder before returning the fan to the conveyor belt. I repeat this hundreds of times a day. Sometimes I work the graveyard shift that starts at six o'clock at night and have trouble staying awake as I drive Dad's car home at two in the morning.

As soon as our combined summer earnings total $600, Jonathan and I purchase a secondhand Ford. Now we can take some girls we like up to Buffalo.

When I return to Moody in the fall, I attend an evangelical church in the suburbs of Chicago. I run into an American friend who married a Gloucester girl and preached at Trinity Baptist Church while getting his doctorate at Oxford.

"How are you doing at school?" he asks.

"I'm on the honor roll."

He looks at me thoughtfully. "With your English education, you could get into an American university!" He doesn't tell me which one.

Mum discouraged me from wanting to go to Oxford, but I'm still ambitious. While his words are fresh in my mind, I notice a list of colleges and universities in the back of my *Webster's Dictionary*.

# Chapter Seven

## *"For God, for Country, and for Yale"*

A quick search in my *Webster's Dictionary* reveals three familiar names. With a shiver of excitement, I send away for applications to Yale, Harvard, and Princeton.

I write to my headmaster at Tommy Rich's to ask for a letter of recommendation. I know he will speak up for me because I was near the top of my class. Since I can't afford to travel to these distant universities, I settle for interviews with local alumni in Chicago. They seem interested. The Harvard Admissions Office indicates I might get advanced placement credit for some of the subjects I passed in the Cambridge exams in England. One of the Yale interviewers says, "You'd better apply for financial aid."

Despite the encouragement, I don't know what to expect and I don't dare tell my parents. I know they will want me to stay at Moody.

To my amazement, I get into all three schools, and by some miracle Yale offers a scholarship for a student "intending to enter the Christian ministry." I will earn part of the money for room and board with a bursary job. Carrying around the precious letter with secret joy, I have no one with whom to share my elation. Quite the opposite! I know only too well this will be difficult to explain to Mum.

After putting it off for a week, I call Johnson Creek to break the news. "I've been accepted at Yale. I'm starting in September."

Dad gasps. "You haven't finished Moody."

Mum takes the phone and jumps in. "That's very deceitful. You didn't discuss it with us."

I hear Dad asking how I'm going to pay for it. I announce that I've won a scholarship.

Their shock and dismay awaken my guilt so I try to reassure them. "I still want to be a minister. Perhaps I could go to Yale Divinity School."

This doesn't help with Mum. She would prefer Moody. But after a stony silence, she guesses that she can't win. She declares, "We'll ask the Lord to find the right friends for you. Don't ever forget—he wants you in the ministry."

Despite her disapproval, I sing inside. What a wonderful country! An opportunity like this would never have come my way in England.

Before I leave Chicago, I attend a reception at the University Club for students planning to go to Yale. Nick Kangas, a quarterback from Lane Technical High School who starred in the public school championship at Soldier Field, has been recruited for the Yale football team. He belongs to the evangelical church that I attend. We decide to room together. Mum says, "It's an answer to prayer."

In the summer, I return to work at Harrison Radiator for a few weeks, and then instead of doing "the graveyard shift," I actually dig graves at the local cemetery. I save my money for a new car. Dad invites me to preach at the Sunday morning service. I love preaching and know I'm good at it.

In September 1956, Dad drives me to Yale in New Haven, Connecticut. It is a grueling trip, but like Eden, where we stayed when we arrived in America, this town's name seems symbolic.

Carrying my Montgomery Ward suitcase, I walk with Dad through a huge tree-lined courtyard called Old Campus looking for my room. We are both awed to find me at Yale. Dad would rather I finished the pastor's course at Moody but is being supportive. Mum, who has not come to settle me in, is angry.

Dad and I go upstairs in Vanderbilt Hall and find I've been given a bedroom with a bunk bed and the surprising addition of a wood-paneled living room with a fireplace. We line up for my sheets and towels from the student laundry staff. I want to reassure him and say, "I'll always be grateful to Moody for bringing me here."

He seems pleased. "That training will stand you in good stead whatever you do."

I'm moved when he holds my arm as he says good-bye. Although he's a warm-hearted man, little physical affection is shown in our family. I can't remember Mum hugging any of us.

My roommate Nick arrives. We put on our jackets and ties excitedly for an orientation dinner in Commons, a vast ornate freshmen dining room, with portraits on the walls of famous Yale graduates like President William Howard Taft. Ben Holden, the university secretary, says, "Congratulations to each of you on matriculating. You are the future leaders of the country."

The director of the glee club leads us in song. "As freshmen first we came to Yale, Fol de rol de rol rol roll." I look around at the singers, a thousand strong—the future leaders of the country. Many of them come from privileged homes and elite boarding schools. I can hardly believe I am one of them. It is glorious! At the end of the evening, we push back our chairs to belt out the alma mater. We wave our handkerchiefs "for God, for country, and for Yale."

Despite Nick's frustration at playing halfback rather than quarterback, he becomes a key man on the freshman team. The other players call him "kangaroo." His ability at football, ready smile, and cheerful personality make him popular, and his friendship and loyalty give me self-confidence. Every evening at six o'clock as we walk to Commons for dinner, the bells of Harkness Tower play a reassuring tune from Dvorak's *New World Symphony*. They remind me of the bells of Gloucester Cathedral I heard so often as a child, and seem to sing, "Going home, going home."

At night we discuss our families. We both have a brother and a younger sister. We laugh when we realize we also have dominating mothers. His wants him to become a doctor so he intends to major in science. I will major in English.

Nick and I join the Intervarsity Christian Fellowship that holds services and a prayer meeting once a week in a small chapel hidden in the base of Harkness Tower. Although the antique choir stalls remind me of Gloucester Cathedral, the prayers are just like talking to God at Moody. I ask the Lord to help me with my studies and to be a faithful witness to the other students. I still feel called to the ministry.

A friend from the Intervarsity Christian Fellowship shares some exciting news. "Billy Graham is coming to Yale in February for a Christian mission." What a surprise! I can't wait to tell Dad, who so admires the evangelist.

On the first day of the mission, someone introduces me to the great man himself. I choke up as I shake his hand and forget to tell him about attending his crusade in England. That evening as Woolsey Hall overflows with serious and eager students, it seems like the rally at Harringay Stadium.

I remember hearing about people criticizing these campaigns as a flash in a pan with no lasting impact. To refute this opinion, I invite the university chaplain, Sidney Lovett, to speak at a follow-up Bible study meeting in our room in Vanderbilt Hall. Over thirty students crowd into our living room as "Uncle Sid" puffs thoughtfully on his pipe and talks about Jesus's calling his disciples. After the meeting, we form several Bible study groups and Uncle Sid suggests we include his associate chaplain, Burt McLean.

Burt McLean not only comes to our next Bible study, but also invites me to stop by his office in Dwight Hall, an elegant red sandstone building in the middle of Old Campus. He has a fire crackling in the fireplace, and I'm immediately attracted to this fellow minister's son, who is a former member of the Yale crew and assistant chaplain of the university. He says he deplores the apathy on campus with regard to urgent national problems. "Last year we tried to organize a lecture series to stimulate debate, but it never got off the ground. How would you like to try it, David?"

Surprised and delighted, I jump at the suggestion. I mail out invitations, but before long each of the candidates turns me down. No wonder that last year the program never got off the ground.

Not wanting to give up, I suggest that if we offer an honorarium of five hundred dollars, we might have more success in attracting speakers. With help from Burt, I organize an alumni sponsoring committee headed by a wealthy graduate named Frank Altschul.

I get recruited myself while clearing tables as a busboy in the Berkeley College dining room. A friendly graduate student, who played rugby at Cambridge and is captain of the Yale rugby team, discovers my experience as scrum half at my grammar school in England. He says, "Why don't you come out to practice?"

"Are there any freshmen?"

"No, but come anyway."

Many thick-necked, muscular football players think of rugby as a form of spring training. Although I feel like Tichy Ball at Tommy Rich's, I have the advantage of knowing more about the game. I may be skinny at 160 pounds, but I revel at getting the ball out fast and tackling hard. One day after practice the captain says, "We need an extra player against Harvard."

My heart pounds with excitement. I'm only a freshman and he wants me to play for Yale against Harvard. The trouble is, the game is at Cambridge, and I have a longstanding date that evening with a girl I met during the summer. She invited me to the prom at Mary Burnham, her boarding school in Northampton, Massachusetts. When I explain my problem to the rugby captain, he replies, "I'll find you a ride."

I borrow a tux from a neighbor in my entryway and pack it with my rugby gear in my Montgomery Ward suitcase. My teammate providing the ride has trouble cramming the suitcase into the trunk of his MG.

Early in the game, as I pass the ball out of the scrum, a Harvard wing forward slams into me and knocks me out. I am helped to the sidelines. Since there is no substitution, the captain wants me back as soon as my head clears. Arriving at Mary Burnham, I still feel groggy from the concussion. The prom has already started. My date points out a small bathroom that is hardly big enough for both me and the suitcase, let alone for changing clothes. It is a major struggle to get on the wrinkled tux.

The dance floor is the next challenge. My evangelical background means I have never danced before, and my head is spinning. I hold my date close, not least to keep my balance. We see the headmistress approach holding a ruler. My date whispers that the school rules require us to remain at least one foot apart while dancing. I notice something on the floor and, trying to distract attention, say to the headmistress, "Somebody has lost something."

"Yes," she replies in a haughty voice. "It's your cummerbund."

From that weekend on I play scrum half for Yale. I proudly clip out a story in the sports pages of the *New Haven Register* describing my twenty-five-yard run to score a try for Yale against Dartmouth.

At the end of freshman year with growing confidence as a Yale man, I return to Johnson Creek ready to flex my muscles. Jonathan and I each put up nine hundred dollars from our savings and trade our used car for a new Thunderbird. We agree to share it in the summer and take turns during the school year.

Dad arranges for me to preach at small Baptist churches scattered in villages throughout Niagara County, where I use sermons I prepared at Moody. He also finds me a summer job as a lifeguard at the Niagara Bible Conference, a camp for boys and girls on Lake Ontario like the Young Warrior camp at Weymouth, but with wooden cabins instead of tents. I introduce Jonathan to a smart, attractive camper named Arlene Hole, and to my surprise their friendship blossoms. I hope the Thunderbird improves my own social life. Like my brother, I want to find a girlfriend.

One Sunday evening my camp roommate and I lie on the grass in front of the tabernacle to watch people walking to the gospel service. A suntanned girl in a white dress walks by with her parents. "Who's that?" I ask.

"Sarah," my roommate replies. "She's got a bad reputation."

In August, the camp director asks me to pick up a new camper who lives in the next village. It turns out to be Sarah. What great luck! With a loose-fitting tank top, skimpy shorts, and bare feet, she later teases me while I wash the Thunderbird. She says giggling, "I love your Bermuda shorts."

Jonathan and I take Sarah and Arlene to the amusement park at Olcott, near the camp. Although the camp director wouldn't approve, I also take Sarah to a drive-in movie theater. She's always laughing. She's such fun.

When I notice two scars in the shape of letters on her arm, I'm shocked. "Why did you do that?" I ask.

She replies cautiously, "They're the initials of my old boyfriend. He works at the gas station."

Sometimes we park in the back of one of the cherry orchards that line the country roads. The fragrance of her perfume and the luxurious leather bench seat make the cockpit of the Thunderbird with its porthole window intimate. We play truth or consequences. I dare her to take off her sweater. She dares me to take off my shirt. She takes off her blouse, her shorts, her bra, and her panties. I also strip everything off. As I lean back in my seat, I feel her naked body pressing down on mine. I've never been so close to a woman. But the inhibitions of my upbringing make me stop short.

On our last night before I return to college, I park my car in her driveway. She seems quiet, almost frightened. As I turn to kiss her good-bye I realize she's crying. She says, "There's something important I want to tell you. I'm going to have a baby."

My heart misses a beat. Sarah pregnant! Am I going to get blamed?

She tells me the father of her baby is her old boyfriend who works at the gas station.

"Do your parents know about him?"

"Yes."

Thank God! Still reeling, I hold her close, trying to comfort her. As tears stream down her face, I realize I care about her very much. I wonder what this will mean to our relationship. I hope the folks at the Niagara Bible Conference don't think the baby is mine.

In contrast to this emotional turmoil, my brother's life seems uneventful. Mum says, "Jonathan has been thinking of going to Buffalo Bible Institute. Why don't you encourage him?"

That evening while Jonathan and I jog down Johnson Creek Road, I suggest, "Bible school seems like a good plan. It might be a stepping-stone to college." He seems to agree.

However, a few weeks later he creates a sensation at the dinner table by announcing, "I want to marry Arlene."

Needless to say, this doesn't go over well with Mum. She decrees, "You attend Buffalo Bible Institute for a year. Then I'll consider it!" Silence descends. Jonathan stares at his plate.

I find a new ally in my sister, Ruth, who has just started high school. Although Mum seems oblivious to Ruth's effort at school, she monitors her daily devotions like a hawk. After dinner Mum and Dad read from the Bible and from a commentary called *Daily Bread*. Then they pray. Ruth must remain at the table.

One stifling evening Mum says, "You pray tonight, Ruth."

"I don't want to," she replies.

"We'll just sit here until you do!"

Ruth, who Mum still hits with a hairbrush, bravely holds out during twenty minutes of silence. Finally, Mum lets Dad pray instead. Ruth tells me, "I don't object to praying. I object to praying on command."

Mum has no plans to send Ruth to college or even Bible school, but I want her to have an opportunity like me. I suggest, "You'd be able to go to college if you improved your grades."

"How?" she asks.

"Do at least four hours of homework every night."

"But I don't have four hours of homework."

"Spend the time reading. Ask your English teacher for a list of classics."

A few days later she shows me a list of three hundred books that she has obtained from the school librarian. "Great!" I exclaim. "Keep a record on your calendar of the time you spend on homework and reading."

We agree she'll send me these calendar records every month. She finishes the reading list and asks the librarian to recommend other books. Her grades improve dramatically. Mum takes it for granted so I praise Ruth for both of us. Ruth and I share an urgent conspiracy to get her into college.

In fact, all three of us children assert our independence in our own ways. Jonathan has already made his move, and Ruth is only just beginning to break away. I still plan to become a minister, but for me rebellion at home leads to triumph at Yale.

# Chapter Eight

## *MARTIN LUTHER KING COMES TO YALE*

As sophomores Nick and I move from Old Campus to Pierson College, one of the residential colleges at Yale. We acquire a new roommate named Larry Bogert, who went to St. Paul's and lives on Park Avenue in New York. Nick calls him "the roomer" because he spends more time with his friends from boarding school than with us. But I like Larry. He's easygoing and he comes from the establishment.

I have discovered that Yale is stratified just like the world I left behind in Gloucester. Yale's pecking order has the men from wealthy and powerful families at the top. High school students from less affluent backgrounds sit at the bottom. This doesn't bother Nick because he was recruited to play football. But it bothers me.

I love Pierson and Yale, but I still feel like an immigrant. I long to escape the narrow social restraints of my childhood and become part of the larger world. When Larry Bogert and his friends from St. Paul's talk about rushing a fraternity, I wonder whether I dare make such a move myself.

I decide to rush Fence Club, which sits at the top of the social ladder. Although my chances are slim, I decide to keep going to the rush meetings as long as I'm invited back. The members of the rush committee seem interested in rugby. I don't mention Moody Bible Institute because I suspect it would not go over well with these affluent young men, but I let them know Larry Bogert is my roommate. To my secret amazement I survive the cut.

I savor the privileges of Fence Club. Long after the Pierson dining room closes, I occasionally linger over the *Tribune* while the steward serves corned beef hash with a poached egg and V-8 juice. What a turnaround from my freshman year when my bursary job was being a busboy myself. This year I run errands for the chaplain's office. I have little in common with the other Fence Club members and don't even have a date for the big parties, but I feel like one of the elite when I wear my Fence Club tie.

In April I stop by Dwight Hall to update Burt McLean on my efforts for the lecture series. He says, "You're a Baptist, aren't you?"

"As a matter of fact I am."

"I've just been reading about a black minister in Montgomery, Alabama, who led a successful boycott of segregated public buses. His name is Martin Luther King Jr."

"I've never heard of him. What do you mean by segregated buses?"

Burt explains, "Alabama law required segregation on the buses. When a soft-spoken black lady refused to surrender her seat to a white person, she was arrested. Martin Luther King Jr. organized a peaceful protest. Thousands of black people walked to work or used carpools to stay off the buses. The revenue of the bus company plummeted, and King was indicted for conspiring to prevent the bus company from operating its business."

"So what happened?"

"A United States District Court ruled that racial segregation on the bus lines was unconstitutional."

"Wow, that's brilliant!"

As I walk back to Vanderbilt Hall I reflect on our conversation. Segregation is foreign to me. There are only five black students in my class, and I had never even met a black person before I came to America. But I love this story of a black Baptist minister who accomplished something important. I decide to invite Martin Luther King Jr. to speak in the lecture series.

In order to broaden support, I persuade my classmates Chas Wood, Tom Currier, and Ambler Moss to join a new student organization that I call the Undergraduate Lecture Committee. I print up some stationery and send off an invitation to Martin Luther King Jr. He promptly agrees to speak in November.

I also invite Walter Reuther, president of the United Auto Workers. Some newspapers suggest Reuther is considering a run for the presidency. Weeks go by with no response.

Hearing former President Harry Truman enjoyed a recent visit to Yale as a Chubb fellow, I send him a telegram pleading for help. To my delight I receive a short letter from Independence, Missouri. "In reply to your telegram, I have sent a note to Walter Reuther urging him to accept your invitation." His intervention makes a difference, and Reuther signs on as our first speaker.

In the summer of 1958, I work as a lifeguard in Tonawanda, New York, to help pay my required share of Yale room and board. Since Tonawanda lies over thirty miles from Johnson Creek, I rent a room during the week from two retired schoolteachers. Mum and Dad give me a ride home on the weekend.

In June, after satisfying Mum with one year at Buffalo Bible Institute, Jonathan marries his strong and capable Arlene. He asks me to be his best man. My life and his gradually diverge. We sell the Thunderbird. It will be a long time before we again join forces.

Shortly after I return to Yale in September, Martin Luther King Jr. publishes a book called *Stride toward Freedom*. To my horror, three days afterward, while promoting the book in a Harlem department store, he is stabbed in the chest. When I write to convey my sympathy, my letter reaches him at Harlem Hospital. He replies, "As soon as I return to my office in Montgomery, I shall consult my schedule to see what dates are available for a visit to Yale. I am sorry that it had to be postponed." Eventually, his secretary reschedules his visit for January.

I buy a copy of *Stride toward Freedom*. It gives me a vivid experience of what it is like to be a black person in the segregated South. I remember how as a child I escaped from bullies in the White City because my dad was a minister. However the fact that Martin Luther King's father was a minister did not protect him for the offensive and demeaning impact of segregation. I have never confronted that kind of insult. I know very little about America, but to be treated like that must be awful. It is easy to empathize with his feeling of injustice.

While I wait for the start of the lecture series, I have a friendly disagreement with Bill Coffin, who has become chaplain. He says, "Fraternities promote the wrong values." He tries to persuade me to resign from Fence Club. I think he wants to use me as part of a political campaign, but I am not about to give up something I prize.

A week before Walter Reuther is scheduled to arrive, I worry about filling the enormous hall. The members of my student committee post placards on the bulletin boards around campus, and there are several stories in the *Yale Daily News*. But is this enough? In desperation I call the mayor's office to extend an invitation to the townspeople of New Haven. Mayor Richard Lee agrees to get the word out and offers to give Reuther a guided tour of the redevelopment underway downtown.

Walter Reuther arrives at the Pierson College master's house looking trim and fighting-fit like a boxer. With a warm smile, he introduces me to a heavyset traveling companion. He says, "We'll need an extra room. He's my bodyguard."

Surprised, I ask, "Why do you need a bodyguard?"

He replies abruptly, "Somebody tried to kill me." Another member of the lecture series at risk! His companion opens his jacket slightly to show me a gun in the inside pocket.

In Woolsey Hall, Reuther talks about finding the proper balance among workers, shareholders, and consumers in a dynamic economy. He says labor and management "have the glorious opportunity of cooperating together to create and share in economic abundance." He receives an enthusiastic reception from the audience. But he gets the opposite treatment from the chairman of the *Yale Daily News,* who writes that although at Yale Reuther preaches "cooperation" of business and labor, he has a different agenda at home. The *News* accuses Reuther of favoring a government takeover of the role of private industry in health, education, welfare, pensions, and defense production.

The debate makes me wonder where I stand on the role of government in society. As I think about it, I realize I prefer less government and more reliance on the marketplace. I believe in freedom of choice and personal responsibility. I remember Dad saying, "People should be encouraged to stand on their own two feet."

The excitement generated by Walter Reuther stimulates a daring idea for another speaker. The newspaper headlines trumpet a proposal by Khrushchev to make Berlin a free city in an attempt to integrate the metropolis with Soviet Germany. Willy Brandt, the mayor of West Berlin, objects strenuously. Why not invite Willy Brandt to join the lecture series?

Since Dad has saved enough for the family to fly back to England for the holidays, I will be halfway there. Full of crazy optimism, I shoot off a letter to the American embassy in Berlin to alert them to my plans.

Arriving in Gloucester, we crowd into Granny Hadley's bed-sitting-room on the ground floor. The Lawn was grander before Grandpa Hadley died. Now Granny rents out most of the house because she needs the income. After fussing over us grandchildren, she pauses to look around. "Where's Irene? Where's my little lost lamb?"

Mum hasn't come straight in. When she does, she doesn't show any emotion. She starts talking about the journey. I can't understand her attitude. She holds back affection from her mother, who she hasn't seen in four years, just as she holds back affection from us.

After Christmas I head for Heathrow. As my plane flies over East Germany, I'm full of misgivings. I grew up thinking of Germans as the enemy. How are they going to feel about me?

When I walk off the plane at Templehof Airport, a young man of my age approaches with his mother. He says he is Hans Albert, a student. He says, "You wrote to the American embassy about your plans and they asked us to meet you. We would like you to stay with us."

Their apartment is modest, but I am amazed how welcome and comfortable they make me. We move around a small undecorated Christmas tree in the center of the threadbare living room.

"Would it be possible to attend church in East Berlin?" I ask.

Hans replies cautiously, "We're free to go between the various sectors, but it is dangerous for people from the West to travel in East Germany."

He agrees to take me to a church called The Dome, warning, "Don't talk on the subway." The sanctuary of The Dome was destroyed by fire during the war, so we join a large congregation worshipping in the crypt. Outside in the Stalinallee, rubble surrounding many buildings reminds me that the people of Gloucester were not the only ones to fear bombs.

At Willy Brandt's office, a staff member asks me, "How many people will come to hear him?"

"About five hundred," I reply, wanting to be conservative.

The staffer rejects my invitation to the mayor. I should have said eighteen hundred, like the turnout for Walter Reuther.

I'm frustrated, but I've had an adventure, and the kindness of Hans Albert and his family has changed my feelings about Germans. When I leave, they give me a German Bible with their names inscribed inside the cover.

My disappointment over Willy Brandt heightens my anxiety over Martin Luther King Jr., who is recovering from the stab wound in his chest. His secretary warns me, "Since his hospitalization, it is necessary that he get at least one hour bed rest every afternoon."

My committee and I wait anxiously for him on the windy platform of the New Haven railroad station. When he alights from the train with a warm, healthy smile, we step forward with relief. He greets us with firm handshakes. We escort him to the master's house at Pierson College, where I have arranged for him to stay, and he joins us for dinner in the Pierson dining room.

I wonder once again if anyone will show up for the lecture. Fortunately, in the evening of January 14, 1959, there is not much going on at Yale. Two thousand people jam into the vast, ornate auditorium packing the balcony and standing in the aisles. The audience is almost entirely white. The term African American is not in everyday use.

Dr. King faces the audience confidently and describes the history of race relations in the United States from the era of slavery to the 1954 decision of the Supreme Court in *Brown v. Board of Education*. The court ruled that separate educational facilities are inherently unequal. Despite the ruling the nation has failed to achieve school integration. It is not only extremists like the Ku Klux Klan, but also state and local officials and even sincere citizens who continue to flout the decision of the Supreme Court.

His voice rings with the authority of an Old Testament prophet as he challenges us to wake up to the shame of this. He urges us to join him in rejecting the monstrous evils of segregation and discrimination. From my seat on the platform next to Martin Luther King I glance at my classmates. Some men stand in the windows on the second floor in order to see him. Others with seats lean forward to focus on his message. No one moves.

His fervent sermon builds toward a climax. He reminds us of Thomas Jefferson who declared, "That all men are created equal, that they are endowed by their Creator with certain inalienable rights, among these are life, liberty, and the pursuit of happiness." He dares us to follow the example of Jesus.

*Undergraduate lecture committee with Martin Luther King at Pierson master's house at Yale in 1959; (left to right) Tom Currier, Chas Wood, David, Martin Luther King Jr., Frank Altschul (alumni sponsor), and Ambler Moss. (Courtesy of Dan Crowley).*

We listen in hushed silence. We have never heard anything like this before. Dr. King tells us that passion and perseverance can achieve integration. It can be accomplished with legal and moral force without violence. Together we can make America truly "the land of the free and the home of the brave."

At the end of his speech, the audience and I leap to our feet applauding ecstatically. People cheer in the aisles. I want to respond, to do something to help America. I hear a call that I do not fully understand.

I had announced a question-and-answer session following the lecture when I introduced Martin Luther King Jr. A huge crowd streams across campus to the Dwight Hall common room. Dr. King sits alone on a couch in the glow of two incandescent lamps. The audience packs into a tight semicircle of chairs around him. The room becomes warm and stuffy, and the eager white faces of the crowd glisten in the lamplight as latecomers pile in to stand three deep in the back. He makes them laugh as he deflects a question about interracial marriage with a smile. He says, "I want to be the white man's brother, not his brother-in-law!"

I don't know all the nuances of race relations, but it seems as if he is not looking to interracial marriage as an answer to racism. At a deeper level, I believe what he really means is that he wants to be my brother.

The next day I take him up to the Divinity School to meet the dean, Liston Pope. On the way back to Pierson College, I remember his secretary's warning and say, "Dr. King, would you like to take a nap?"

"That won't be necessary," he replies. "I never expected to spend my thirtieth birthday at Yale!"

I quietly purchase a cake with fancy icing and candles and round up my student committee. We gather in the Pierson master's house. Martin Luther King Jr. laughs in surprise when we march in and sing "Happy Birthday." As I help him cut the cake, someone snaps a photo of us.

During the three days he spends with me, he asks about my family. I say, "My dad's a Baptist minister."

"Then we have something else in common," he replies. "Mine is too!"

I tell him I want to write a paper on desegregation in the schools, which might involve traveling to Alabama to gather information. On his return home he writes, "I hope our paths will cross in the not-too-distant future. If you decide to come to Montgomery, please let me know and I will do all that I possibly can to make your visit enjoyable." I feel honored.

*David helps Martin Luther King, Jr. cut his birthday cake on his thirtieth birthday on January 15, 1959, at Pierson master's house at Yale.*

He sends me a carbon copy of his lecture with corrections to the text in his own handwriting for inclusion in a future booklet of all four lectures, to be edited by my classmate Jack Heinz. The lecture is also published in the *Yale Alumni Magazine*.

His words continue to reverberate in my mind. He is an evangelical like Mum, but he is also active outside the church. He seems to combine political activity with a life of integrity, peace, and determination. Perhaps he meets Dad's ideal of living "in the world but not of the world." I want to be like him.

Should I switch my major to political science?

# Chapter Nine

## *A Major Change of Direction*

I decide to test my instinct on Burt McLean about switching my major. As the pendulum of a grandfather clock ticks back and forth in his office in Dwight Hall, I explain, "I admire Martin Luther King Jr. as a spiritual person who is politically involved. I want to know more about his ideas for influencing change."

The assistant chaplain doesn't seem at all surprised and nods his head sympathetically. He says, "Many men really take off once they discover their real interests in life."

With his encouragement, I tell the chairman of the Political Science Department I want to write a research paper about desegregation in schools following the 1954 Supreme Court decision in *Brown v. Board of Education*. Few black students have been admitted to historically white schools. The chairman approves my new major.

My research takes me to the law school library. I soon discover that before the Brown decision, segregation was required by law in seventeen states and the District of Columbia. Response to the decision varied from prompt and complete desegregation in the District of Columbia to determined resistance in the Deep South. Virginia adopted a program of massive resistance and closed some schools rather than be forced to integrate. North Carolina adopted a policy of token integration, and a handful of black students were admitted to mixed public schools. Alabama and some other states adopted a pupil placement law, which enabled local authorities to use criteria like the psychological qualifications of the pupil to control admission of black students without being openly discriminatory.

Recently in *Shuttlesworth v. Birmingham Board of Education*, 358 U.S. 101 (1958), the Supreme Court upheld Alabama's Pupil Placement Law as not unconstitutional on its face. This seems to weaken the Brown decision. I would like to find a way to challenge pupil placement laws in the courts.

I don't mention the change in my major to Mum because I don't want her to get upset. After all, I still plan to become a minister, but feel the pull of the world of political science.

The lecture series moves into high gear when Henry Ford, chairman of the Ford Motor Company, signs on as the next speaker. The company faces difficult bargaining with the United Auto Workers over a new three-year contract, and Henry Ford, a member of the class of 1940, wants to answer Walter Reuther.

In order to reserve the auditorium, I need to obtain the approval of the university secretary Ben Holden. To my surprise, he sends me upstairs at Woodbridge Hall to chat with President Whitney Griswold. The president welcomes me with a purposeful look, but starts by inquiring where I prepared for Yale and about my career plans. With a benevolent smile he says, "I've noticed that the sons of ministers and doctors tend to follow in their fathers' footsteps."

Soon he gets around to Henry Ford. He asks me to bring Mr. Ford over at two o'clock on the day of the lecture. He adds conspiratorially, "Would you mind if I discussed something with him privately?" Of course I don't have much choice but wonder what is so important.

When Henry Ford arrives at Pierson, I offer to carry his bags up to his room in the master's house. He refuses abruptly. I get the impression he doesn't want people fussing over him. But he warms up when he discovers I've borrowed an old Model A to publicize his visit and offers to drive me around campus. The *Yale Daily News* runs a picture of him chatting with me next to the Model A.

*Undergraduate lecture committee advertises lecture of Henry Ford (left to right) David, Chas Wood, Tom Currier (with Yale bulldog Handsome Dan IX), and Ambler Moss at the wheel of a Model A Ford in 1959. (Courtesy of Dan Crowley).*

On the day of the lecture, I deliver him to Woodbridge Hall for his mysterious appointment with the president. An hour later, Ben Holden greets me exuberantly. "David, you've done the university a great favor! My classmate and friend Henry Ford never graduated from Yale, but he has agreed to head up the alumni fund drive in Detroit."

A big crowd gathers in Woolsey Hall to hear Mr. Ford argue that excessive union wage demands have an inflationary effect. He says, "The best way to increase economic growth is to bring the economic and political power of unions within reasonable bounds."

Our last speaker arrives in March. Former Congressman Brooks Hays discusses "An Alternative Method of Desegregation." Mr. Hays had arranged a meeting between President Eisenhower and Governor Faubus of Arkansas in September 1957 to try to resolve the crisis over the admission of black students to Central High School in Little Rock. After eight terms in Congress, he was defeated for reelection by a write-in vote for a segregationist. A smaller crowd turns out for Brooks Hays, but the average attendance for the four lectures is 1,800 people.

As a result of the crowds and extensive coverage in the *Yale Daily News,* I have become well known on campus. The student publisher of *Ivy Magazine* compares me to a famous producer of events in the performing arts. He says, "You are the Sol Hurok of Yale University." This happens at a time when members of the junior class, like me, hope for a bid from a senior society.

The six senior societies at Yale generate a great deal of curiosity among undergraduates because of their "tombs" or windowless mausoleum-like buildings scattered on valuable real estate around the campus. Each of them taps fifteen members of the junior class. Nobody knows what happens in the tombs because society members never discuss their activities. This lack of information encourages wild and sometimes ridiculous speculation. The *Yale Daily News* reports that the six societies have designated the third Tuesday in April as tap day.

The oldest and most venerable secret society is called Skull and Bones. Several seniors in Pierson are members, including Winston Lord, president of Fence Club, who lives in my entryway on the floor below. On tap day, as the bells of Harkness Tower chime five o'clock, I wait in my room with my loyal roommate Nick. Suddenly, Winston Lord bursts in and slaps me on the shoulder. "Skull and Bones! Do you accept?"

"Yes!"

He hands me a piece of paper and rushes out.

Loyal Nick laughs good-naturedly. He knows we mustn't discuss it, but he understands my joy without anything being said. Inside I sing the "Hallelujah" chorus! I'm an immigrant from England, the son of a humble nonconformist minister, who has just entered the inner circle at Yale, a world where everything seems possible. I've never been so happy.

I'm still singing when I return to Johnson Creek for the summer. Dad announces another reason to celebrate. "We've been here five years. We're eligible to become citizens." Mum, Dad, Jonathan, my fourteen-year-old sister, Ruth, and I drive to the federal courthouse in Buffalo to be sworn in. As the judge congratulates us, I feel grateful and proud that they came with me to America and we can share this inspirational moment.

In the lottery for rooms for senior year, my roommates and I draw a luxurious wood-paneled suite with a fireplace in a small whitewashed Pierson courtyard ironically known as "the slave quarters." Nick becomes a celebrity when he returns a kickoff ninety-eight yards to win the Princeton game. I work on getting to know my classmates in my senior society. All I need now is a good-looking girlfriend.

One of my new friends, David Holbrook, an art history major with an interest in politics, invites our group to lunch at his parents' manicured estate in Bedford, Westchester County. David's attractive younger sister, Phyllis, happens to be in New Haven for the weekend, and he asks me to give her a ride to Bedford. I feel pleased to be asked but tense. She chats about her three brothers, who all attended Yale. I'd like to see Phyllis again, but I think someone with her background is unlikely to be interested in an impoverished student like me. Lunch unfolds as an elegant occasion served by a well-trained staff and presided over by David's formidable mother. I glimpse a world of affluence I've never before experienced.

I reach out tentatively for that golden world when I buy a tux at Brooks Brothers on Madison Avenue to wear at a dinner for the New York members of Skull and Bones. As I part with the last hundred dollars of my summer savings, the English foxhunting prints on the store walls—symbols of the British establishment—seem to affirm the wisdom of this extravagance.

The dinner is held at the University Club in New York. I sit down between Henry Luce, founder of *Time Magazine*, and Averell Harriman, former governor of New York. I know Henry Luce's parents served as missionaries in China.

"Were your parents with the CIM?" I ask. He can't believe I've heard of the China Inland Mission. I explain how we supported it at Dad's church in England.

Henry Luce turns to Harriman. "Do you know what the letters CIM stand for?"

Harriman mumbles, "I have no idea!"

Luce and I exchange a smile. I remember uneasily the famous English cricket player C. T. Studd, who gave up everything to be a missionary for the CIM. I had to memorize his motto to earn the Young Warrior's badge at chapel. As Mum pinned that Young Warrior's badge on me, she whispered, "When you were born, I dedicated you to the Lord's service."

I shake off this ghost from the past and concentrate again on the conversation around me. Averell Harriman leans across me to discuss with Henry Luce the nearing end of Dwight Eisenhower's second term as president. "Do you regret supporting the constitutional amendment that prevents Ike from running for a third term?"

Luce snorts, "No! It's healthy to have a change."

Waves of excitement shoot through me as I sit between these two famous men discussing national issues, but I try to act as if it's an everyday occurrence. I would love to be important like them.

The remarkable dinner has stimulated my imagination. Although I think I'm now free of Mum's domination, I discover a tension between planning to be a minister and a vague new aspiration to be a leader in the establishment.

During the fall, I spend hundreds of hours in the law school library, working on my research paper. I pore over pupil placement laws in Alabama, Louisiana, North Carolina, and Virginia and reports of actual integration in *Southern School News*. Very few black students have been admitted to integrated white schools.

I find a case called *Yick Wo v. Hopkins*, 6 U.S. 1064 (1886). In 1880 San Francisco passed an ordinance making it unlawful for any person to maintain a laundry in a wooden building without securing a license from the board of supervisors. The ordinance appeared to be quite fair. But in the six years that the ordinance had been in operation, while other applications were granted, no Chinese laundryman had received a license. In ruling in favor of Yick Wo, the Supreme Court said,

> Though the law be fair on its face, and impartial in appearance, yet, if it is applied and administered by public authority with an evil eye and an unjust hand, so as practically to make an unjust and illegal discrimination between persons in similar circumstances, material to their rights, the denial of equal justice is still within the prohibition of the Constitution. (*Yick Wo* 6 US at 1073)

Fired with enthusiasm, I develop a thesis that although pupil placement laws are not discriminatory on their face, they may well be discriminatory in their application. In time it should be possible for black children to bring a class action challenging the laws as violating the equal protection clause.

As I emerge into the sharp air and go down the steps each evening, lights glimmer in the Gothic fortress of Sterling Memorial Library across the street. Sometimes I miss dinner, but I feel satisfied with the work done and very happy. An intriguing idea grows. Why not apply to law school? This would constitute a monumental change in my plans. I think about that moment at Tommy Rich's when I told the headmaster I wanted to enter the ministry. Did I really want it, or could I think of nothing else after Mum had eliminated farming and Oxford? Did the desire come from her rather than from my real self?

I'm not sure. The ministry still beckons. When I see Dean Liston Pope at a party organized by the *Yale Daily News*, he encourages me to apply to the Divinity School. Since my friend Burt MacLean has left to become headmaster of a school in Hawaii, I turn to Chaplain Bill Coffin for advice. I assume he will encourage divinity school too, which is what I want.

But the charismatic and controversial chaplain gives me a serious look. "If you can possibly do something else, don't be a minister."

What a shock!

I ask, "What do you mean?"

He replies, "It involves great sacrifice, and you need to feel called by God."

Having grown up in a church home, I know what it entails just as well as he does. I would be fulfilled by many aspects of the ministry, especially preaching and counseling people. I certainly don't worry about sacrifice.

When I pick up my mail at Yale station, I see an advertisement for a scholarship program offered by the Rockefeller Brothers to students considering seminary, but who are not yet sure about their calling. This seems to fit my situation. But do I really want to continue down the path of the Young Warrior? Bill Coffin has swayed me and wider ambition pulls. Dreaming of leadership in the larger world of business, law, or government, I consider applying to Columbia Law School.

New York City promises adventure. As a resident of New York State, I qualify for financial aid, and if I continue to work as a lifeguard, I can save enough money to pay my share of tuition, room, and board without any help from my parents.

I'll do it!

I break the news during spring vacation. Dad must have seen it coming. Supportive as ever, he says, "You'd make a good minister, but I'll be proud of you as a lawyer. We certainly need Christian laymen."

Mum turns away, silent for a moment. I sneak a look at her face. It seems to be without emotion. Finally, she declares levelly, "You've been led astray!"

But I don't feel led astray at all. I vow to help make the world a better place in a secular career.

Many of my classmates also have big dreams. Several of us talk about our aspirations over lunch at Zeta Psi fraternity, including a man who sat next to me in French class named Bart Giamatti. He describes his plans for graduate work in comparative literature and talks about his fascination with Milton's *Paradise Lost*. We both assume that our earthly paradise in New Haven will extend into the unknown future. Bart confides, "Despite all the jokes about wanting to be president of the American Baseball League, my real ambition is to be president of Yale."

Mum makes no further comment about my plans, although she decides to come to Yale with Dad to attend my graduation. I count on them for a ride home. To my surprise, she is in a cheerful mood. Perhaps she's over her disappointment. After the ceremony in the sunshine on Old Campus, she suddenly announces she wants to drive to New York to attend a crusade by Billy Graham in Madison Square Garden. I have no choice. She's plotting to get me back in line.

We arrive in time for the evening rally, and a friend of mine from Moody gives us some seats near the front. As Mum hopes, the drama of the crusade and the certainty of Billy Graham's message again make me feel the tug of the ministry. Dad stays on for some meetings, while Mum and I drive five hundred miles through the night to Johnson Creek.

Despite the clever maneuver, she hasn't shaken my conviction that I've graduated from Yale on a magic carpet. I'm setting out with the rest of the class of 1960 to run the country.

# Chapter Ten

## *My Glimmering Girl*

After working all summer as a lifeguard in Tonawanda, New York, I nervously pack my battered old Montgomery Ward suitcase for law school. Looking around the living room at the parsonage, I notice a small plaque sitting on top of the television set, with a quote from a Christmas broadcast by King George VI at the beginning of the war. It says, "Go out into the darkness and put your hand into the hand of God. That shall be to you better than a light and safer than a known way." The words sound reassuring.

I ask Mum, "Would you mind if I took it with me?"

"Of course not," she replies, smiling.

I move into a bleak monklike cell in a graduate dormitory at Columbia on 115th Street in Manhattan. I struggle with first-year classes and, like most of the other students, study long into the night. Although I would never admit it to Mum, I am better prepared for the ministry than for the law. I feel out of place in the law school's competitive atmosphere. One of my worldly classmates sees the quote from King George VI standing on my chest of drawers. He says, "Hey, what's that? You religious or something?" I try to ignore the put-down.

At night I kneel beside my bed and ask the Lord for help and guidance. On Sunday mornings I set off on an urgent search for a church home. I try an evangelical church led by a preacher I heard at Moody, as well as the Riverside Church and the Episcopalian University Chapel.

Thank goodness for my friend David Holbrook. He welcomes the other side of my personality. He works for Marsh & McLennan and lives with his wife Holly on the fashionable East Side. I take the bus down Riverside Drive, grateful for an invitation to dinner. With a transfer, the journey takes well over an hour, but it costs only fifteen cents. As David pours a glass of Chateau Margaux in their elegant apartment, I describe shivering in the bitter cold wind on the corner of Eighty-Sixth Street while waiting for the crosstown bus.

He says, "You should take a taxi. They're cheap." But he doesn't understand. A taxi would cost a dollar and a quarter. I don't have that kind of money.

Once a week we play squash at the Yale Club. Often we go back to his apartment for a gourmet dinner prepared with flair by Holly, who embraces me like a family friend. To my delight, they ask me to be godfather for their first child, Helene.

Their warm hospitality continues when I return to school in September 1961. I move to International House on Riverside Drive with other students studying in nearby graduate schools. Half are from abroad and half are American. I fit into both categories.

My room has a dramatic view of the Hudson River, almost down to the place where our ship docked when I arrived in America. Some of my fellow students volunteer for the Peace Corps President Kennedy establishes. Below my window I can see them in Claremont Park steaming through push-ups and jumping jacks, getting fit in preparation for service abroad.

The Peace Corps volunteers prompt a long discussion during lunch in the cafeteria with Dr. Taylor, the vice president of International House. We admire the aspirations of the Peace Corps, but Dr. Taylor has noticed how young people can start out with great idealism and then give up because they discover they can't change the world. I wonder out loud whether for most of us it would make more sense to follow the example of Dr. King with the Montgomery bus strike, to try to change just that part of the world where we can make a difference.

The friendly administrator invites me to be president of United Nations Week. Our guest of honor is Eleanor Roosevelt. However, the most important person I meet is Morganne Arnold from Long

Beach, California. She catches my imagination, blond and tall with the warmest, most open smile I've ever seen.

She tells me about working for her master's at the Columbia School of Library Science. I challenge her to a game of table tennis. Laughing when she misses a shot, she makes me feel like a champion. I invite her to the movies.

It's snowing and she shivers a little as she grabs my arm to shelter beneath an umbrella. As the bus rattles down Riverside Drive, she recites a poem by Yeats. The poet catches a silver trout with a hazel wand. While he prepares the fire, something mysterious happens to the trout.

> *It had become a glimmering girl*
> *With apple blossoms in her hair*
> *Who called me by my name and ran*
> *And faded through the brightening air.*

Whatever the poem means to Morganne, it seems encouraging she wants to share it with me.

Just before the movie starts, she asks shyly, "Did you notice that I wear contact lenses?"

"No," I reply, wondering if this means she cares what I think. The lights dim. I take her hand.

As the forsythia bursts into blossom, we explore Riverside Park and meet for evening snacks in the cafeteria. She went to Mills College in California, but took her junior year at Bristol University, only thirty miles from where I grew up in Gloucester. She giggles at my stories of going to the Bristol Zoo to see my favorite animals: Alfred the Ape and Rosie the Elephant.

More seriously, I tell her about Martin Luther King Jr.'s lecture in Woolsey Hall. He talked about the decision of the Supreme Court in *Brown v. Board of Education* and the need to mobilize behind school integration. I describe how his lecture inspired me to major in political science, and that in turn led to my decision to go to law school. I say, "I vowed to help make the world a better place in a secular career."

She gives me a wide-open smile. "I feel the same way." She radiates sympathetic warmth. I have never met anyone quite so wonderful.

Our friendship seems to deepen. Then suddenly, she suddenly cuts it off. Every time I call she turns me down. Wretched, I don't understand what went wrong. She disappears from my life, just like the mysterious glimmering girl in the poem by Yeats.

Her rejection makes it hard to concentrate, and I stumble through courses in commercial transactions and accounting, in which I have no background. I fail them both. Making them up requires an extra semester to graduate. I return to Johnson Creek for the summer confused and depressed. But I still don't want to concede I made the wrong choice of career.

Feeling miserable, I drive to Mahwah, New Jersey, for the wedding of Dick Lindgren, one of my Skull and Bones classmates, to Anne, his college sweetheart. On the spur of the moment after the reception, I swing into Manhattan to spend the night at International House. Although I hear Morganne has gone on vacation with her parents, I decide to talk with one of her friends in the somewhat unrealistic hope of getting her back.

To my amazement, her friend says cheerfully, "Morganne's here. She'd like to see you!"

Morganne comes down from her room with a big smile, and I can tell the magic has returned. I cautiously invite her to go shopping with me the next day. She readily accepts and my confidence grows by leaps and bounds. Walking up Fifth Avenue, I ask, "Why did you give me such a rough time?"

She laughs. "It was good for you!" But the chemistry of our relationship has changed, and she grabs my hand as if it is she who is chasing me, and not me chasing her.

I want to see her again soon. This poses a challenge because I have a job in western New York while she attends summer school at Columbia. She agrees to fly to Johnson Creek to visit me. On the day of her arrival, I have to work in Tonawanda, so I ask my parents to meet her at the Rochester airport. I hope they take a liking to each other. Dad takes her cherry picking on a farm belonging to one of the members of his congregation. When I walk into the parsonage, she greets me with her wide-open smile.

Her naturalness charms Jonathan, Ruth, and even the curious farmers at church on Sunday. She seems at home with country folk.

Most important, it is evident that her unassuming manner pleases Mum.

We walk along the creek in the woods and lie down in a field frothy white with Queen Anne's lace. Morganne teases me about my Brooks Brothers attire at International House. "I like you better in a T-shirt. You look more natural." I realize to my chagrin that my need to look good almost made me lose her. She explains what happened in the spring. "I was afraid you were from an affluent background where I wouldn't fit in." Her eyes sparkle. "I like you more now that I've seen you in your natural habitat!"

She tells me about her family. "Mom is a librarian. Pop is a mailman and never graduated from college. They were childhood sweethearts in the Depression. They didn't want to have a baby."

She draws a deep breath. "I don't like knowing I was an accident!" She laughs, but it seems like an effort.

For a moment she gazes up at the clouds lost in thought. "I had dozens and dozens of babysitters, mostly navy wives. Some were good. I kicked the awful ones. Things got better when I was eleven and my father's mother, Grammie Arnold, came to help. My friends liked her and started to hang out at our house." She shakes her head. "But my mother still left for the library just when I got home from school."

To my surprise, Morganne tells me she was miserable at Bristol University. "I missed the California sunshine. My roommate wasn't interested. One day I lay in the snow to see if anyone would come to rescue me. Nobody did."

She pauses and sits up, looking off at the woods in the distance. "I fell in love in my senior year at Mills. My friends were jealous because Vim was good-looking and mature. Mom and Pop liked him. But then he told me he was already married and had a baby. He wanted to continue our relationship because his wife was mentally ill." Her face crumples with the pain of the memory. "I thought he loved me, but someone who loved me wouldn't do that, would they? I almost dropped out of college."

Breaking off a stalk of grass, she bites the end. "At Columbia I had a boyfriend in my class. I thought he loved me too, but I guess I wasn't good enough for him. He dumped me for another girl. I was still going to a psychiatrist at Columbia for help when I met you."

I take it for granted she has recovered from her history of depression and all will be well. Her honesty and vulnerability only make her lovelier.

I take a deep breath and say, "I love you."

To my great joy she replies, "I love you too."

She offers to pay for my plane ticket to visit her family. I can hardly believe our friendship has gone so far.

After she picks me up at the Los Angeles airport, we drive along a highway lined with pink and dark red oleander. Brilliant sunlight makes me think I've landed in an enchanted foreign country. We arrive in Long Beach at a white ranch house with black shutters on a street lined with unfamiliar palm trees. I'm impressed with its tasteful interior of oriental carpets, comfortable wing chairs, and shelves of books. Morganne has put a vase of roses in every room.

Moments later, a loud voice jars the magic kingdom. Her mother yells from outside, "Morgan, help unload the car!" She is tall with dark curly hair and seems very much in charge.

Later I ask Morganne why her mother calls her Morgan.

"She named me after Morgan le Fay in Malory's *Le Morte d'Arthur.*"

"What was Morgan le Fay like?"

"Horrible. I like Morganne much better."

"Pop" Arnold has receding blond hair and a dry sense of humor. He says, "The trouble with women is they're always trying to make you over." When I walk his mail route with him, he entertains me with stories about the residents, the dogs, and the post office bureaucracy. He calls Morganne "Mouse."

Morganne wants to take me to San Francisco with her kindly Grammie as a chaperone. But her mother overrules, insisting, "I'll take you!" As we follow El Camino Real to visit the old Spanish missions along the coast, we all sing, "This land is my land. This land is your land."

At Big Sur I have some moments alone with Morganne. In the blazing heat of the sun, we race across the sandy beach and stand to catch our breath at the top of a steep cliff looking down at the incoming tide. We say we don't want to be separated again. I ask, "Will you marry me?"

As the waves crash, I search her face, anxious for a moment, but her eyes are filled with tenderness. She says, "Yes! I'll come back to New York. If I can't find a librarian's job, I'll be a waitress."

Our parents give us their blessing, but both mothers decree we should wait a year before getting married.

Morganne finds an apartment with another girl on Riverside Drive and starts working in the young adult department of the New York Public Library. Her laughter bursts like warm sunshine on Morningside Heights. She teaches me to greet people with a breezy California "Hi." I return to law school elated and confident. I enjoy courses on federal taxation and subchapter S corporations. Perhaps because of my familiarity with sin and punishment, I excel in criminal law.

We spend our evenings together in her living room. She lies on the couch and rests her head on my lap, like a small child needing to be held. With her encouragement, I write weekly letters to Mum and Dad. On Sundays we share a hymnbook. I have found a soul mate.

Morganne's mother flies to Johnson Creek to meet my parents. She says to Mum, "I love the old cobblestone houses and the farming community, but I'll bet it's a struggle. You must have a lot of potluck dinners to raise enough money to keep the church going."

Mum believes that Christians should give at least ten percent of their income to the Lord's work. She retorts, "We don't potluck, we tithe!"

However, by the end of her visit they get on well. Mum says with satisfaction, "Your daughter has given me back my son."

# Chapter Eleven

## *Starting a Family*

Mum, Dad, and Ruth travel across country by train for our wedding on August 28, 1963, at St. Luke's Episcopal Church in Long Beach, California. Two of my classmates, who happen to be stationed with the military on the West Coast, serve as groomsmen. Jonathan flies in to be best man. We revel in a sun-filled, joyful reception on the church lawn. I wish it could go on forever.

When we return from our honeymoon, we move into a low-rent, one-bedroom apartment on Riverside Drive at 108th Street. Morganne goes back to the New York Public Library. After her first day at work, she shows me an old newspaper and exclaims, "Can you believe this? On our wedding day, Martin Luther King Jr. gave the keynote address at a massive demonstration in Washington in support of a civil rights bill. Over two hundred and fifty thousand marchers, white as well as black, filled the Mall from the Lincoln Memorial to the Washington Monument. There was not a single negative incident. It was like a gigantic picnic."

She sits next to me on the couch to study the paper. A few moments later she blurts out, "He believes that all that matters is the kind of people we are, not what we look like." She turns to me with tears in her eyes. "I feel the same way."

We share a concept of a better world. This is something we can do together. I reach over and squeeze her hand and manage to say, "Me too."

Morganne bustles about the tiny kitchen, proudly organizing our meals and joking about the occasional cockroach. She enjoys her job but worries about safety. Each night I take the subway to library branches all over Manhattan and the Bronx to escort her home.

Marriage transforms my experience of Morningside Heights. As I walk up Riverside Drive to the law school in the crisp early morning, the leaves are turning to red and gold. I write in my diary about a miracle—this lovely person has chosen me. When I see a mailman, I make a point of smiling and saying, "Hi," thinking of Morganne's dad. Study comes easy. I get my best grades.

In our seemingly endless honeymoon, Morganne and I are pleased to hear from Mum. She has received an electrifying letter from Dulcie, wife of her brother Peter, who went to Australia when he was sixteen. Dulcie says their son Geoffrey, a Methodist minister, has entered Union Theological Seminary only a few blocks from where we live. Mum wants me to get in touch with him right away.

Delighted at the chance to meet a cousin from Australia, we visit Geoff and his wife, Lillian, in their apartment on Broadway at the edge of Harlem. Geoff tells me with a grin, "Granny often went off to the Electricity Board in London, leaving her children to fend for themselves. Your mother, who was the eldest, had to prepare the meals. My dad says that while he was growing up she was his best friend."

It sounds pretty grim with Granny away. I wonder what else he knows that I don't know.

We quickly fall into a routine of dinner once a week with the Hadleys, followed by bridge. Geoff describes how Granny Hadley once traveled all the way to Australia to see her son Peter. He says, "She came on a luxury liner with a male companion who was not her husband. Dad told me she called him Bert."

Startled, I ask, "What was that guy Bert doing with her?"

"He was an old friend of the family from the Gloucester Rowing Club."

"Did your father know him?"

"Yes. Granny and the children used to visit his bungalow at Elmore on the canal."

Geoff chuckles. "Dad was twenty-seven, living in a primitive farmhouse and milking cows by hand early in the morning and late in the afternoon, every day of the year. Granny tried to persuade him to abandon his wife and baby—namely me—and return with her to England."

I gasp. "How appalling! What did your father say?"

"He took her to the dock at Fremantle and never saw her again!"

Mum invites Geoff and Lillian to visit Johnson Creek over Thanksgiving, and Dad asks Geoff to preach on Sunday. He tells the congregation about the challenges of farming in Australia. When we sit down to lunch in the parsonage, he adds, "It must have been hard for my father to give up his comfortable life at The Lawn."

Lillian turns toward Mum and exclaims, "Isn't it curious your brother Peter never wanted to go back to see his family in England?"

"I'm not at all surprised!" snaps Mum.

Lillian seems taken aback.

I wonder what made Mum say that. She never explains. In fact, she never talks about her childhood, as if those years have been obliterated from the history books. I know Granny went off to London. But was it more than that? Did something traumatic happen to drive Peter and Mum away?

While I ponder these questions Mum and Dad travel to England to visit her family. A few weeks after their return, Mum receives a cold, shocking telegram from her sister. "Mother died this morning. Heart failure. Joyce."

Dad tells me Granny had a problem with nosebleeds. Just before they left, Mum had taken Granny for a walk up Tuffley Avenue and confronted her about a sinful affair in her past and her need to get right with God. I wonder, when Mum receives the telegram, how she feels about this last interaction with her mother. Ruth says, "She didn't show any emotion at all."

I don't understand why she sheds no tears for her mother. Come to think of it, she didn't cry when her father died. Something went wrong in their relationship. But I don't know what it was and I don't dare ask her. It will be a long time before I learn the family secret.

I am searching for a job. I turn up the business card given me three years earlier by a friendly lawyer. He is a partner in the Wall Street firm of White & Case. With a mixture of daring and apprehension, I make an appointment to see him. Fortunately, he remembers me and insists

I return for an interview with the hiring committee. This means five busy partners, including the chairman of the corporate department, who pepper me with questions about subchapter S corporations.

After work that night Morganne asks, "How did it go?"

I reply, "I don't know. It was rough. I just about exhausted everything I could remember from my course on subchapter S corporations."

The following week I receive a letter offering me a job with a starting salary of $7,200. Morganne hugs me gleefully. "You're too modest, David! You must have dazzled them with your learning."

The office occupies four floors of the Bankers Trust headquarters at 14 Wall Street, near Trinity Church and across from the members' entrance to the New York Stock Exchange. The firm has over one hundred lawyers, making it the third largest law firm in the country. As at Brooks Brothers when buying my tux, I see foxhunting prints in the hallways. I feel I'm entering the establishment.

However, my work is not glamorous. Five new lawyers start with me. We cram into a tiny office called the bullpen, with five desks and one window. We research questions assigned by partners on the front line and spend long hours in the library slogging through case after case.

I hear Martin Luther King Jr. has been nominated for the Nobel Peace Prize. Just to be nominated is a huge tribute, and he is only thirty-five—the youngest person ever proposed for the award. I feel proud of him and proud that the world is recognizing his leadership for social change. He made a difference in his small part of the world in Montgomery and now he has set his sights on passage of the civil rights bill.

I am particularly excited that the legislation picks up the problem of pupil placement laws that I researched in college. Back then I cited the case of *Yick Wo v. Hopkins* to argue that although pupil placement laws were not discriminatory on their face, they may well be discriminatory in their application. I eagerly follow the bill through Congress and am elated when President Lyndon Johnson signs it in July, with Martin Luther King Jr. at his side. The act authorizes the federal government to desegregate public schools. Now the Justice Department can initiate lawsuits and assume much of the burden of litigation.

Riots break out in Harlem, Brooklyn, and Jersey City. Civil rights workers are murdered in Mississippi. But when Martin Luther King Jr. is awarded the Nobel Peace Prize, he reiterates his belief in nonviolence. I hope his way will prevail. The growing militancy of some black people scares me.

One evening when I walk into the apartment after work, Morganne runs to meet me. Her face is flushed with excitement.

"Guess what? My doctor told me I'm pregnant."

I joyfully take her into my arms. "You don't feel any different to me."

"I will soon!"

She quits her job at New York Public. As a celebration, she reads me Tolkien's *The Hobbit* in the evening.

In February 1965 we read in *The New York Times* that Martin Luther King Jr. has gone to Selma, Alabama, to support the registration of black voters. In many parts of the South, poll taxes, literary tests, and other devices are used to disqualify black people. They make up 60 percent of the population of Selma and the surrounding county, but only a few of the voters are black.

Dr. King leads over two hundred protesters from Brown Chapel in Selma to the local courthouse to register. We are shocked when the Nobel Prize winner and everyone with him are arrested for marching without a parade permit.

On March 7 a group of demonstrators defy an order from Governor George Wallace and start a march in protest from Selma to the state capital in Montgomery. Morganne and I watch on television as the demonstrators cross the Edmund Pettus Bridge. Horrified, we see state troopers beating them back with night sticks and tear gas. Morganne buries her head in my shoulder.

I cringe as unarmed people are hit and clubbed. They run coughing, crying, and vomiting through the gas cloud—because they are black. Only because they are black and asking to be treated the same as other citizens. The injustice of it is monstrous.

A few days later, three white Unitarian ministers are brutally beaten after bravely eating in a black-operated restaurant. One of the ministers dies without regaining consciousness. President Johnson addresses a rare joint session of Congress and denounces the "crippling legacy of bigotry and injustice." He promises to submit a bill that will guarantee voting rights to all citizens.

We religiously keep up with the news. On March 21, Dr. King leads protestors on a fifty-four mile march from Selma to Montgomery. He speaks triumphantly to a crowd of twenty-five thousand people in front of the state capital building. He refers to the savage attempt to stop the march on the Pettus Bridge and defiantly declares that he and the protestors will not be cowed.

Morganne and I need to make a move ourselves. Now that she is pregnant, we want to find a home where we can raise a family. With financial help from Morganne's grandparents, we buy a co-op apartment at 55 East Seventy-Sixth Street near Central Park. It occupies the seventh floor of an old brownstone, with a shaky elevator and floors that sag, but has an extra bedroom for a baby.

Once we settle into our new home, Mum announces she plans to visit. Knowing her, she will look in every cupboard. This causes a problem because Morganne and I occasionally enjoy a glass of wine. When I was a child, Mum pledged to the Women's Christian Temperance Union that I would not touch strong drink while under her care. I have no doubt she considers wine to be just as bad as strong drink, and she certainly thinks of me as under her care.

We decide to put the wine into a large cardboard box, seal it with tape, and label it BOTTLES. The subterfuge works. We repeat it whenever Mum looms on the horizon.

# Chapter Twelve

## MAKING A DIFFERENCE IN THE BIG CITY

After one year in the bullpen at White & Case, I move to the tax department. One of my first assignments involves drafting an amendment to increase benefits under the Bankers Trust Company pension plan. I travel uptown with one of the partners to meet the chairman of the bank in his spacious office on Park Avenue. The chairman says, "We can pay for the increase with the surplus in the plan."

I take a second look at the financial statements. To my surprise, the plan has a huge unrealized gain on its investments.

For the first time I begin to think about pensions. What a difference one would make to Granny Hadley, now living frugally by renting out most of her home. And another memory comes sharply to mind.

When I was a boy, Dad used to take me to visit an old lady named Miss Philips. We went up dark stairs to her damp one-room apartment in an area of Gloucester that flooded. The worst thing about these visits was trying not to gag. The building reeked from the constant stink of a nearby factory that reduced bones to make soap.

I asked Dad, "Why does she live here?"

"It's all she can afford," he said. "Life is hard when you're old and have very little income."

I felt sad for kind Miss Philips.

As I tackle my new assignment, it seems increasingly worthwhile. I remember how Martin Luther King Jr. quoted Thomas Jefferson in Woolsey Hall. "All men are created equal and are endowed by their creator with certain inalienable rights, that among these are life, liberty, and the pursuit of happiness." Good modern pensions can help create happiness and financial security for older people.

While I learn about pensions, Morganne starts frenetically cleaning, scrubbing down every wall of the apartment. She even scrapes paint from old wooden bed frames left behind by the last owner. But I have to finish the project when she suddenly becomes anxious about exposing her baby to the fumes of the paint remover.

On June 16, 1965, she has a difficult labor requiring general anesthesia. When the doctor comes to the waiting room to tell me we have a son, he adds soberly, "I had to use forceps to deliver the baby." But Morganne writes gleefully to her godmother, Blanche, "He's a sweetie—looks like his father—dark hair, blue eyes, pointed chin, and squashed nose." We name him David Jr., and call him Davy.

In August, as we delight in our baby, *The New York Times* reports that President Johnson has signed the Voting Rights Act. The new law empowers the attorney general to send federal registrars into counties where there is evidence of discrimination. Once again Dr. King has made a difference.

Davy often cries in the night and Morganne becomes exhausted. On Saturdays I take him for a walk in the stroller in Central Park so she can have some time off. We watch the model sailboats on the boating lake and visit the zoo. As the months pass Davy learns the names of the animals. When we return home after a stop for a milkshake, he demonstrates to his admiring mother that he has learned to drink with a straw.

*David with Morganne and Davy at Johnson Creek in 1966.*

Morganne never complains about my long hours at White & Case, but one evening a power cut plunges all the buildings in Manhattan into darkness. The phone rings in my pitch-black office. I fumble around to pick it up. It's Morganne. "When are you coming home?"

"Sweetheart, I'll be on my way as soon as I can find someone with matches to show the way downstairs."

"I was taking a bath when the lights went out." She sounds nervous.

"Are you okay?"

"I groped around naked until I found some candles."

"Is Davy okay?"

"He's asleep," she replies. "Please come home soon!"

I feel my way down twenty-eight floors in the dark and then struggle up Broadway with thousands of other stranded workers, guided by car headlights. It takes two hours to walk from Wall Street to Seventy-Sixth Street. Just before I reach home sweaty and exhausted, the power comes back on.

Morganne meets me at the door and I hold her. She jokes that she's made a fuss about nothing, but she looks strained. I remember her history of depression. I need to be more mindful of the stress in her life.

We organize activities for young people at St. James, our neighborhood Episcopal church. When a black preacher gives the sermon, we chat with him at the door, hoping he will feel welcome among us. He says, "My church in Harlem is called St. James too. I'd love to have you come and visit." We drive up to St. James and sit in the middle of the congregation. We are the only white people.

As we return home Morganne exclaims, "I'm glad we went. But it was quite a shock." She hesitates to reflect a moment before she continues. "I wish we could do more than go to church in Harlem."

I reach over to squeeze her hand. "We must find a way to make a difference."

A note from a classmate named Charlie McCarthy, who has become assistant director of admissions at Yale, presents an opportunity. He asks, "Would you be willing to serve as a mentor for a black student who attended the Yale Summer High School Enrichment Program?"

I'm delighted to be able to do something practical and write back, "I'd love to. Please put me in touch."

His name is Gerald Edwards. We invite him to lunch and Morganne makes a special seafood salad. Gerald tells us he's near the top of his class, plays baseball for the school, and loved the summer program. Since he's obviously very bright, I say, "Why don't you apply to Yale? I'll write a letter of recommendation."

Morganne backs me up with encouragement. Gerald begins to smile as he realizes it might be possible.

The application goes off. In April Gerald calls. His voice is full of the same excited wonder I felt when I got the news. "I've been accepted."

"Come over for lunch," I tell him. "We need to celebrate." It is gratifying that one more black student will be added at Yale. We spend three hours talking about how I went as an awkward recent immigrant but ended up with some great friends. We walk him to the bus stop and promise to visit him in New Haven.

In his freshman year, Gerald seems much like the young man we first met, but when we return in his sophomore year, we are amused to discover he has decorated his room in Styles College with wooden crates and hung fish netting from the ceiling. However, we are all concerned about race relations.

Morganne asks, "What do you think about the riots and the dangers that James Baldwin describes in *The Fire Next Time*?"

"I'm pessimistic about the future," he replies.

She shakes her head but tries to be positive. "Martin Luther King Jr. believes in nonviolence. He has shown us the way."

On the train back to New York she tells me, "I would like to leave Gerald something in my will."

As usual, I'm touched by her generous spirit. "That's a lovely idea, sweetheart."

She adds, "And one day I want to do something for America."

"Yes, yes, we both will!" I feel blessed to have a partner who shares my desire to help make the world a better place.

We decide the best way to help is to get involved in politics. Local government has been dominated for years by the Democratic Party machine at Tammany Hall and the city has become almost ungovernable. One of my professors at Yale, who had worked in city hall, said the way the previous mayor, Robert Wagner, used to run the city was to read the morning newspaper and that would determine his agenda for the day.

We accept an invitation from David Carls, a friend in the bullpen at White & Case, to campaign for John Lindsay, a Republican congressman running for mayor. We believe this charismatic graduate of Yale College and Yale Law School will bring good government, restore order, and fight for social justice. He's a reformer and an idealist like Martin Luther King Jr. This is something we can do for America.

Morganne accepts an invitation to lunch with Mary Lindsay and gets caught up in the political campaign. At first we both work on the phone bank at the Republican Club of the Ninth Assembly District on Eighty-First Street. But after a while she says, "I don't have the stomach for cold calling," and quits.

I continue on my own. I wish Morganne would change her mind, but I'm fighting for both of us. As election district captain, I distribute campaign material in the apartment buildings in our neighborhood. I become even more deeply involved when David Carls persuades me to sign on as assistant treasurer of the club.

On the day John Lindsay becomes mayor, the head of the Transit Workers Union calls a strike. This shuts down the subway and creates chaos. I hear John Lindsay urge on the radio, "Unless you are indispensable, don't try to go to work today." I get the message and stay home. But later I find out that everybody else at White & Case went to work.

David Carls chortles, "We wondered if you were dispensable!" I could kick myself!

But I make a comeback when I'm invited to serve on the Mayor's Task Force on Tax Policy. I obtain a month's leave of absence to work with John Lindsay's chief of staff and a team of lawyers drafting legislation to reform the city tax structure. We target the city's myriad "nuisance" taxes for abolition. I help design a new levy modeled on the state income tax. I believe the reform will help make the city tax system more fair and equitable.

After we complete our assignment, the mayor invites everyone to a party at Gracie Mansion. Morganne and I stand in the sunlight on the porch overlooking the river, while John Lindsay sits on the rail chatting with members of the task force. He says to me with a warm smile, "How would you like to help collect the new income tax?"

Cautiously, I reply, "For the moment I want to stay at White & Case."

I try to stay involved by agreeing to serve as treasurer of the Republican Club. At the same time, my assignments at White & Case become more demanding. Ambition drives me to accomplish everything with impossible perfection. I get headaches and the muscles in my back seize up. My doctor puts me on Valium.

Morganne becomes pregnant again, but at night patiently rubs my back to help me relax. She says, "Put your hand on my tummy. You can feel the baby move." What a miracle. With my hand resting there waiting for the next kick, Morganne and our baby seem much more important than my career.

On March 13, 1968, we are blessed with the gift of another son. He is a sweet and placid baby who takes readily to breast-feeding. We call him Christopher.

Morganne, who with dancing eyes once said, "I want six children with mild chaos all around," begins to worry about raising a family in New York City. She exclaims dejectedly, "There's nowhere safe for the children to play. And where will Davy go to school?" She wants a house with a yard for the children.

I assume she'd like to move near her own family in the California sunshine. Although I could ask White & Case for an introduction to a Los Angeles law firm, I hesitate to raise the matter for fear of jeopardizing my job. But she's lost that wide-open smile, and I must choose between my career and her happiness. I decide to ask the head of the tax department for help.

That evening when I tell her what I have done, she throws her arms around me. "David, I don't want you to give up your job." I hold her tight, amazed at her loyalty and warmed by her love.

We investigate neighborhoods within commuting distance of New York. For the first time since I left England, I realize I miss the countryside of Gloucestershire. Morganne likes a wooded lot with a stream in the back country of Greenwich, Connecticut. So do I. It reminds me of the bluebell wood at Grandpa Ball's farm.

We hire a local architect to design a house that looks like the George Wythe house we admired on a trip to Colonial Williamsburg. We drive out on weekends to check on the work. In the spring we cuddle under the plywood of the unfinished roof and listen to the rain falling softly in the woods.

On a blazing hot summer day, with the stream glittering in the sunlight, Morganne jumps impulsively into the three-foot-deep water. Though snapping turtles cross my mind, I join her. She has taught me to be more spontaneous. As we laugh and splash, I long for her to stay happy.

# Chapter Thirteen

## *MOTHER'S DAY*

While the builder starts digging the foundation of our new home, we read a disturbing report in the *New York Times* about looting and gunfire by black people dissatisfied with Martin Luther King Jr.'s policy of nonviolence. He is now a contentious figure not only to white opponents of his ideas. His charismatic leadership enrages everyone who wants to prevent his influence. I think of the knifing that delayed his coming to Yale and the bomb thrown at his home. Morganne says, "I hope and pray no more anger will be turned against him personally."

He travels to Memphis, Tennessee, to help sanitation workers in a strike against unfair labor practices. I later learn that in a sermon at Mason Temple, a Memphis church, Dr. King tells the congregation about his flight from Atlanta that morning. The pilot apologized for a delay because of a bomb scare.

With steady sincerity, Dr. King addresses the crowd in the Mason Temple. He offers a realistic assessment of the situation. Despite the personal danger, he is happy. He does not know this is his last sermon.

The next day, April 4, 1968, as I listen to music at home, the program is interrupted by a terrible announcement. I stare frozen at the dark wooden radio. Martin Luther King Jr. has been shot and killed.

Martin Luther King Jr. is dead.

An icy wave of sadness sweeps over me. I have lost the kindred spirit who has inspired me since those three days we spent together at Yale. I shudder at the brutality of his murder. And close after the shock comes fear of what violent horrors may follow.

Morganne is devastated. She writes to her godmother, Blanche, "You told me once if we could ask for joy from life then we must also be willing to accept the pain. But now the pain seems on us all. Only in watching and holding Christopher does life seem peaceful."

Nightmarish scenes fill the television: riots, burning, and looting in black ghettos across the country. I read in the newspaper that the rioting in Washington is the worst in the capital's history. President Johnson declares a national day of mourning.

I think about Dr. King's Memphis address. It is comforting to know he was happy. In fact, it is wonderful. He was happy because he had inner strength and conviction that what he was doing was right. I wish I had it. What am I going to do now? I am still searching.

Morganne continues to brood as we prepare for the move to Greenwich in August. Our house is not ready, but our apartment is sold and we must go. As she struggles to keep the children clear of the carpenters, plumbers, and electricians, she becomes increasingly strained. During my lunch hour, I anxiously slip into Trinity Church to pray for her.

One hot, sticky weekend I hear her banging around upstairs. When I go up to investigate, I find the chest of drawers pulled open and a pile of clothes heaped on the bed. "What are you doing?" I ask.

She replies firmly, "I want you to take all these to the collection center in Manhattan for the people of Newark who have lost their homes in the rioting."

It takes me hours to find the warehouse on the lower West Side. I am glad we can contribute and humbled by her willingness to do without my help for a big chunk of the day. The aftermath of Dr. King's murder weighs heavily on me too, but Morganne has done me a favor in reminding me that we must carry on.

I still believe we can make a difference in politics like John Lindsey. We join the Greenwich Young Republicans. I arrange for a speech to the group by Jim Linen of *Time Magazine*. As she did in the Ninth Assembly District in New York, Morganne once again feels out of place and unhappy in the cut-and-thrust political atmosphere. We drop out, and with a twinge of sadness I realize politics will have to wait.

After a drizzly Saturday cooped up at home, Morganne sits despondently at the kitchen table. She sighs, "I don't have any friends." Davy, now five, reaches over and puts his hand on her arm.

I try to reassure her. "You do have friends. What about Debby, Ingrid, and Carol Keefe next door?" But none of them seems to satisfy her.

On weekends, Davy follows me around while I build stone walls or work on a concrete dam across the stream. Sometimes he builds stone walls himself with wooden blocks, using his toy telephone to call the lumberyard. It makes us laugh to hear him say, "Hello, Mr. Bunny. Do you have any concrete?"

He talks all the time and asks a lot of questions. However, he finds it hard to concentrate. Morganne tries to teach him to read flash cards, but he has trouble recognizing the words. She gets impatient and snaps at him.

She says, "I'm making the same mistakes my parents made with me."

"What do you mean?" I ask.

She doesn't explain. I don't know what those mistakes were, except that her mother used babysitters all the time. But I notice Davy always clings to me when I return home from work. He seems desperately glad to see me.

The assassination of Martin Luther King Jr. makes us determined to find a spiritual home in the neighborhood. Morganne finds a place for us at St. Barnabas, a newly established mission in the back country. At Lent she cautiously ventures out with me to dinner meetings in the elegant homes of parishioners. She says, "What I like most is the unpretentious feeling in the worship service."

In early 1969, one of my clients at White & Case—a small company called Southeastern Public Service Corporation—offers me the position of general counsel and corporate secretary. I know the management fears a takeover by an unfriendly shareholder named Victor Posner. However, it offers me a chance to leapfrog ahead since it would take another five years to make partner at White & Case.

As I consider the offer, I remember someone saying at Yale, "We're renaissance men. We can do anything." I think, *Perhaps the raider can be blocked.* With visions of saving the company, I grab the opportunity and attend my first board meeting.

My euphoria doesn't last long. Victor Posner continues to purchase shares on the open market and within six months he amasses over 50 percent of the outstanding stock. His lawyer and accountant arrive at our corporate headquarters at 70 Pine Street and sit in the conference room facing me down. I feel like crawling under the table.

Victor Posner asks me to stay on, but since he has a questionable reputation, I resign. I wonder if I've run out of luck. Perhaps I made a mistake in leaving White & Case. I barely have enough cash to last three months. How am I going to pay the bills? I come down with the flu, which lingers on week after week. Unemployed and stressed-out, I lose my temper at the muddles at home.

We find a babysitter and escape to the Mayflower Inn in Washington, Connecticut, to discuss what to do about my future career. I settle in a comfortable old chair in the corner of the bedroom. Morganne perches on the edge of the bed and says, "David Ball, listen to me! You've become cranky and opinionated!"

This stops me cold. I think of my impatience and my social ambitions. They have an impact on her. I swallow. "I'm sorry. I'll really try to be more considerate."

Immediately, she gives me her sweet smile. "I forgive you. I understand the pressure you're under."

After the scare at Southeastern, I jump for a safe job as assistant general counsel of The Babcock & Wilcox Company, with an office in the Chrysler Building near Grand Central Station. Thanks to a shorter commute, I get home in time to tell the boys a story and hear them say their prayers.

One thing I like about Babcock is my return to the world of pensions that intrigued me at White & Case. Once again a surplus in the defined benefit plan enables management to consider an increase in benefits. I work with the actuaries to determine the cost of the amendment. I also serve on the committee administering the plan, where I find employees with long service and big salaries receive large pensions, but those who leave before they vest get nothing.

A friend from St. Barnabas who happens to work for Babcock tells me, "I feel trapped. I've been offered another job, but I'm hanging on to get a pension." His remark leaves me disillusioned. I discover for the first time that under a traditional defined benefit plan, employees who change jobs can lose most if not all their pension benefits. I wish I could do something to help.

Apart from my fascination with pensions, I find little to enjoy in my new job. Instead of the excitement of policy decisions at board level, I wrestle with contracts to sell huge boilers for power plants. I travel to the Babcock plant in Barberton, Ohio, to learn about the unfamiliar world of power generation. I get headaches and backaches, and my osteopath recommends sleeping on a heating pad. Sometimes I have nightmares about boilers. How could I be so wrong as to think of myself as a renaissance man? As Morganne patiently rubs the tightness out of my back, I wonder whether I should have entered the ministry after all. I wouldn't have much money, but at least I'd have the satisfaction of helping people with their problems.

Morganne doesn't seem so healthy herself. She says, "I feel tired all the time." She wonders whether she has a sinus infection.

She enjoys Christopher so much we decide to have another child, hoping this will give her joy. It seems to work. She writes to Blanche, "A year ago I was depressed and wondered if it was all worthwhile. Today I feel full of thankfulness for a loving husband, two lively and wonderful boys, another child coming, and this comfortable, dear house." Her nose-and-throat specialist confidently predicts her sinus problem will clear up once she has the baby. I hope he's right. I want to believe she can recover the joyful spirit of our honeymoon.

Uncomfortable and frazzled at the end of her pregnancy, she invites Mum to care for the boys while she is in the hospital. What a relief for all of us when Mum breezes in with all the self-confidence of Mary Poppins. On Sunday instead of joining us at St. Barnabas, she insists on us taking her to an evangelical congregational church in Stamford. That's just like her. But we're glad for her help.

Morganne wants a girl but expects another boy. After a short, easy labor the doctor says, "It's a girl." She doesn't believe him and has taken out her contact lenses, so he shows me the baby for confirmation.

"Yep, it's a girl!" I declare proudly. We call her Deborah, a biblical name meaning honeybee.

Morganne cradles her baby with a deep glow of pleasure. I gratefully think, *We have two boys and a girl, just like my parents. Mum is pleased too. Debby was born on April 16, Mum's birthday.*

We hire Marianne, a baby nurse, to help for a few weeks. However, Morganne, exhausted and overwhelmed by the enormous burden of her responsibilities, asks Marianne to stay on indefinitely.

She persuades her own godmother, Blanche, to fly out right away and serve as godparent for Debby. We also corral my classmate Bob Giegengack, a geology professor at the University of Pennsylvania, and his wife Fran. After the baptism at St. Barnabas, the rector joins all of us for a festive lunch at home. A few weeks later, when the rector invites me to serve on the vestry, I say to a beaming Morganne, "Thanks for finding St. Barnabas."

I develop new friendships at vestry meetings, but Morganne grieves when a longtime friend, whom we knew in New York, moves away from Greenwich. To make matters worse, her mother writes that one of Morganne's childhood buddies in Long Beach, who had a small baby, has committed suicide by jumping off a bridge. My glimmering girl seldom laughs anymore.

As winter comes and the days darken, she sighs. "I seem to be sick again. If my sinuses don't clear up soon, I'm going to get them washed out." She often seems bewildered by her inability to cope. She writes to my brother's wife, Arlene, "I never worried with two, but somehow with three and all there is to do—trying to become organized and keep my health—I've gotten so tense that my stomach is knotted up."

I look forward to that moment after the children have gone to bed when she reads books to me. But one blustery night as she reads Tolkien's *The Lord of the Rings* and describes Frodo's stumbling in agony up the rocky slope of Mount Doom, her pace slows and her voice drops. She whispers, "Sometimes the trees seem dark and foreboding. I feel like Frodo." The wind howls outside and I shudder in alarm.

Winter drags on. We continue to grapple with colds and the flu. Her contacts bother her, so she starts wearing glasses with a black frame that make her look even more washed out. The doctor suggests her sinus problem might be allergies and refers her to an allergist who starts a treatment of weekly shots. She says, "I feel better after the shots, but a few days later I seem to become more depressed."

Debby thrives with our capable baby nurse who even offers to help with some of the light housework. But one evening when I come home from work, Morganne confesses, "I blew up at Marianne. I hit her. It was awful. Later on I apologized."

"What made you do it?" I ask.

In a subdued voice Morganne replies, "She makes me feel so inadequate."

Her confession tears me apart. I don't know what to say, but I hope it's an isolated event. Then it happens again. I suggest, "If you can't get on with Marianne, perhaps we should let her go."

Neither of us knows where to turn. She tells me apologetically, "My allergist has suggested a psychiatrist named Dr. Morley." I don't have a lot of confidence in psychiatrists, but I feel relieved when she begins weekly visits to the doctor. She has no energy and withdraws within herself as if she is just trying to survive. We place a bed in the library so she can rest quietly in a darkened room during the day. She says, "I'm useless. I'm ready for the wastebasket." As I hear her wounded cry and see the lines on her pale white forehead, I feel helpless too.

Confused and distressed, I start calling Mum and Dad just to chat. After fourteen good years in Johnson Creek, they have moved to a church in Attica, New York, where they feel appreciated. Although I find our conversations comforting, I don't tell them about my fears.

Morganne's fits of explosive anger grow more frequent. One morning I walk into the kitchen to sit down for breakfast. She suddenly flings a bowl of cornflakes over my head. I don't know why. I'm too startled and hurt to ask. Another time, she does the same thing to Davy when he won't eat his cereal. Once, when I arrive home from work, she says, "I threw a hammer at Davy. You can see the marks on the wall."

Horrified and helpless, I don't know what to do.

In March, hoping the sunshine will help restore her health, we fly out to California to visit her parents and her godmother, Blanche. But while Pop Arnold drives us to visit a family friend, she gets into an argument with her mother. "You thought your career in the library was more important than taking care of me!"

Mrs. Arnold snaps back, "I had no choice! Bob worked at the gas station and we had bills to pay."

As the argument intensifies, her father turns to me and suggests, "Why don't you two get out and walk home, so we can all cool off?"

In a calmer moment, we discuss what to do about our baby nurse. Our perfect nanny seems to undermine Morganne's self-esteem. We decide to let her go at the end of April hoping that Morganne will feel better in the spring. Just before I climb into the car to leave Long Beach, her father says sympathetically, "You've got a big problem on your hands!"

Morganne has trouble sleeping and pleads, "Get into bed and hold me." Like a broken recording machine, she talks over and over about her mother, about not having any friends, and about not being able to cope. I tell her, "You do have friends and family that love you. You can cope without Marianne." With my arms around her I pray, "Heavenly Father, please give Morganne assurance of your love." I believe God can hear me, but as she goes on and on in the same baleful voice, I'm scared.

Early on Sunday morning, I dash out to pick some violets in the woods. I make a pot of tea, boil an egg, and butter some bread. With a little prompting, the boys march into the bedroom carrying the violets in egg cups. Davy declares proudly, "Happy Mother's Day!" I nestle Debby on the bed next to her mom with a Mother's Day card. Morganne beams with pleasure as they hand her their gifts. She says, "Thank you so much. I was hoping you'd bring me breakfast in bed!"

On Monday night when I tell Morganne my boss has given me a raise, she smiles. I take her proudly into my arms, give her a kiss, and lift her in the air. She says, "You're so capable, David!"

We walk to see the horses across the lane, and I tell her of my concern about her unhappiness. As we return to the house, I say sadly, "I wish I was more capable as a husband."

She shakes her head. "You *are* a good husband, David! This has nothing to do with you."

It doesn't make me feel better. My stomach churns at work the next day, and, returning home in the evening, my hands sweat on the steering wheel.

Once again she has trouble sleeping. I climb into her bed and cuddle her while she pours out her pain. I listen until I can barely stay awake and then crawl back into my own bed. I glance at the alarm. It's two o'clock. Completely exhausted, I fall asleep.

# Chapter Fourteen

## *An Empty Bed*

The alarm shrieks at seven o'clock on May 11, 1971, and as I shuffle to the bathroom I notice Morganne's bed is empty. She often goes ahead to make breakfast for the children. I glance through the bathroom window to see a police car pull into the driveway. A sickening premonition hits me. I rush downstairs in my T-shirt and shorts.

When I open the front door, I find two policemen. One of the officers says, "Someone reported seeing a woman park a station wagon on the Tappan Zee Bridge and climb over the rail. The wagon was registered in your name."

I realize I've invited them into the library. They sit facing me. I stand clutching the back of a chair while a voice says, "We believe your wife jumped or fell from the bridge."

The policeman pauses. I shiver, cold and vulnerable in my underwear. Chill spreads through my mind and my heart. I struggle to get hold of what's happening. "Did anyone see her jump?"

"The motorist didn't say," an officer replies.

"Could she still be alive in the water?"

"They're looking for her."

"Should I go?" I ask in the fleeting hope I can do something to help.

"There's nothing you can do. They'll notify you as soon as they find her."

I think if they haven't found her, she might still be alive. I ask, "Could she have just walked off the bridge?"

"It's possible."

The officer continues in a suspicious tone, "Do you have any idea why she might have done this?"

"She was suffering from depression."

"Was she taking any medication?"

"Yes, antidepressant pills. She had a prescription from a psychiatrist."

While we talk, the phone rings. "This is the *Daily News*. Do you have any comment on the report your wife jumped or fell from the Tappan Zee Bridge?"

I don't know what to say. I blurt out, "Try to understand how someone feels when they've lost the person they love."

The police ask for the antidepressant pills and leave abruptly.

With a sharp pain in my stomach, I check on the children. Debby is asleep in her crib. The boys in their baby-blue pajamas tell me they pursued Morganne downstairs and saw the station wagon disappear out the driveway. Now they sit on the floor playing with their Fisher-Price airport. I stagger back upstairs and fall to my knees by my bed with tears streaming down my face. I whisper, "Lord, help me."

Fumbling blindly for the phone, I call Dad. "If ever I needed you, I need you now!"

Dad doesn't hesitate or, for once in his life, stop to consult Mum. He knows she'll feel the same. He says, "We'll come right away."

Numb and dazed with my eyes still blurred with tears, I stumble over to our neighbor's house next door. Carol Keefe offers to help, so I tell the children, "Mrs. Keefe is going to take care of you."

Instead of going to work, Dan Keefe walks with me round and round the house and through the wood. Tears running and running, I tell him about Morganne and her depression. I sob. "How could this happen when we loved each other so deeply? How could she abandon the children and me? Why didn't God answer my prayers?"

I'm afraid to call Morganne's parents. I don't want to have to tell them their daughter has committed suicide, so I call her godmother Blanche instead. She gasps in horror.

Mum and Dad arrive in the late afternoon. They must be in shock too. Mum hugs me as she walks in the kitchen door. She's never done that before. She takes over caring for the children. Davy is five, Chris is three, and Debby is one. While Mum holds Debby, I sit in the rocking chair in the kitchen with Davy and Chris on my lap. With a catch in my voice and my face wet with tears, I say, "Mommy has gone to be with God."

In the morning I discover a short story about Morganne in a box on the front page of *Greenwich Time*. I slam the newspaper down on the kitchen table in dismay. How could they make a feature out of her death? The police are still searching for her. With a sudden burst of anger, I throw into the trash can the old diary I began in England. Dad, who happens to notice, asks, "Are you sure you want to do that?"

"I won't need it anymore," I reply in a thick voice. But later on I wish I could recover what I wrote about Morganne. I buy another notebook. The only way I stay in touch with life is by writing down what happens to me and what I feel.

Dad goes back to Attica because he has a church to lead. Mum stays. How reassuring to have her running the house and taking care of the children.

After a week I return to Babcock & Wilcox, only vaguely aware of other people. I lean over my desk and bury my head in my hands. As one day runs into another, I lose consciousness of the outside world, but the bitter emptiness inside goes with me everywhere. Night after night I fall on my knees to ask God for help.

In the bleak early morning, Mum feeds Debby, who squeaks a little, but I would rather stay here in the kitchen with them than be alone. She says, "Poor, dear Morganne! She must have been very ill not to know how much we all loved her."

Mum pauses to give Debby another spoonful of baby food. She continues, "When you called us so often lately, we had no idea how worried you were." I've never known her so sympathetic.

I start a new paragraph in my notebook. "Morganne taught me how to love and how to give. She healed my relationship with Mum."

I tell the children Morganne can hear them when they pray. The next day Christopher finds me working in the garden. He says, "Daddy, let's pray to Mummy." I lift him onto my knee and close my eyes. He prays, "God bless Mummy and Daddy, Davy and me, and baby. Amen." He leans against my cheek in the warmth of the sun. It seems, for a moment, as if she is present, caressing us, loving us.

I dream she really didn't jump off the bridge but simply kept walking to the other side. As I wander along Fifth Avenue in New York, I see her face in the crowd. A couple of times I hear her car come in the driveway. I turn to the window, but there's no one there.

Morganne's parents, Bob and Zee, arrive. They've lost their only child. They've lost part of themselves. They seem stunned and don't talk much.

Two weeks go by and the police still have not found Morganne's body. Dad suggests we go ahead with a memorial service at St. Barnabas. The rector reads from the Twenty-Third Psalm, "Yea, though I walk through the valley of the shadow of death, I will fear no evil: for thou art with me; thy rod and thy staff they comfort me." I want to hold on to that promise.

It helps to remember the Bible story of Job. In the face of unbearable suffering, he cried out, "Though he slay me, yet will I trust in him."

The next day, the phone rings, and an impersonal voice says, "This is the New Jersey State Police. We think we've found your wife's body. We need someone to provide identification." The news snuffs out my last flickering hope. I shudder in horror. All that remains is a ghastly trip to the morgue. I can't do it. I ask her parents to undertake the grim assignment.

Zee and Bob keep to themselves until we gather at Putnam cemetery. The funeral director hands me a small metal can containing Morganne's ashes. As I kneel down, I bury part of myself in the ground with the can. I'm an actor in a silent movie. The rector mouthing the words of the committal has no voice. The dusty black earth has no moisture for my hands. The white sun has no burn. The dry cemetery grass has no smell of death.

Bob and Zee always supported our marriage. Now Bob's friendship is rock solid, and Zee doesn't seem critical. She says, "Morganne's illness may have been postpartum depression. My grandmother suffered so badly from postpartum depression, she had to be hospitalized after the birth of each of her children."

But all her sympathy cannot bring back my glimmering girl. Morganne's spirit, in the warmest, most open smile I've ever known, has flown away. My grief stays trapped inside.

Tormented by guilt, I pray over and over, "Lord, forgive me for letting her down." I ask myself, "What if we hadn't moved to such an affluent area where Morganne didn't fit in? What if we hadn't gone through the stress of building a new house? What if I hadn't been so ambitious in my job and left her alone so often? What if we hadn't let Marianne go?"

Desperate for answers, I seek out Dr. Morley, Morganne's psychiatrist. He says Marianne's departure may have been the trigger for Morganne's suicide, but she had a depressive personality disorder. "She didn't receive enough love as an infant and child. She felt unwanted and rejected."

"But she knew I loved her," I insist. "I was always saying how good she looked, what a difference her warmth and love made in my life."

"David, she couldn't hold on to that belief," Dr. Morley says gently. "Ultimately, she turned every situation into a negative one."

I put my head in my hands. I sob with the hopelessness of it. "Would she have been better off marrying someone else?"

I look up at Dr. Morley. He shakes his head solemnly. "No one could have given her infinite love. If I had had any idea she was suicidal, I would have put her in the hospital."

Like a guardian angel, Blanche comes to visit. She listens patiently while I pour out my anguish and my sense of failure. I tell her Morganne eluded me, like the glimmering girl. She says, "I'll never forgive Bob and Zee for the way they treated her as a child."

She shows me a letter that Morganne wrote from the Mayflower Inn in January 1970. She had written, "My, I'm glad that I married him."

After her visit, Blanche writes with more comfort. "For you there will always be the knowledge of all you and Morganne have shared, and for us the gratefulness that you helped her so much. Thank you for choosing her and loving her and wrapping your fates together. You will always be richer for it, just as she was wonderfully rich in having you."

Gradually, my focus shifts from the cold reality of the empty bed next to mine to the sad, white faces of Davy, Christopher, and Debby. I begin to confront a staggering problem. After Mum returns to Attica to live with Dad, who will take care of my children?

At first I hope it will be my sister Ruth, who is now married and living in England. She flies over with her English husband Jim. They wonder if they should move to America to help. I arrange some interviews and Jim gets several job offers in New York.

The children like our visitors. Davy joins Ruth on a wooden bench under the maple tree. They hear a little bird calling in the branches overhead. Ruth asks, "What do you think he's saying?"

Davy solemnly glances up at her. "He's looking for his mother."

His words almost persuade Ruth to take on the responsibility. I would be thrilled if she did, although I worry about her giving up her way of life. I say, "For you to be happy, it should be for your own sakes as well as mine."

After talking it over with Jim, she reluctantly responds, "We'd really prefer to live in England."

Their decision propels Mum into action. She insists Dad resign his pastorate in Attica so they can take care of their grandchildren. They're both sixty-four years old. What a huge sacrifice for my family and me! What a relief to have them take over. But despite my gratitude, I can't help feeling invaded as they move their furniture into my house.

Mum bustles around the kitchen making a pot of tea while Davy sits at the table looking glum. She glances over at him. "We all feel sad, Davy, because your mother died, but we have to keep going!" She offers me a cup of tea and tells me her memory of meeting Morganne for the first time. "She sat on the couch and kicked off her shoes, just as I do. I thought, *My, I'm going to like you!*" And she did.

Auntie Vera and Uncle Gerald come to visit. When Auntie opens her suitcase, ripe gooseberries tumble out. She says, "I expect you'd like some Oldbury tarts." I stare with astonishment at fruit from Kington Mead Farm she has managed to bring through customs without difficulty.

Ever loving and helpful, she kneels on the floor to polish the brass claws on the legs of the dining room table. She says, "My father was in the same predicament as you when my mother died leaving him with four small children. It must have been hard for him." She stops polishing to look up at me. "Still, he managed. We were happy children."

It comes as no surprise that before long Mum tries to draw me back into her church and her world. Once, after I go out to dinner with some Yale friends, Mum asks, "Why were you so late last night? I couldn't get any sleep." I don't reply, but I bristle with anger. She has no right to say that. She's trying to direct my life once more.

Gradually, an atmosphere of silent disapproval grows as she becomes aware of my lifestyle. She objects to bottles of wine that Morganne and I once carefully hid from her, and to my wasting so much money on pachysandra for the borders around the house. Just as she has done so many times in my life, she declares, "You're not pleasing the Lord." Since I appreciate her taking care of the children, I try to ignore her accusations, but she leaves a sting. Auntie Vera, who is an evangelical Christian like Mum, would never say anything like that. Why must Mum be so severe?

In October the pastor at the Evangelical Congregational Church in Stanford resigns, and Dad agrees to serve in his place. He thinks he should move into the parsonage near the church, but Mum wants to stay with me. I encourage her to move with Dad because I need to prevent her from being "mother" in my grown-up, independent household. I suggest she could have Debby, while I keep the boys.

Mum has grown particularly close to Deborah in the five months since Morganne's death. Perhaps baby Debby reminds her of the abandoned baby she rescued and cared for on the mission field in India. She makes plans to join Dad at the parsonage and take Debby with her. She tells the people at church, "The Lord wants me to take the place of her mother."

I soon realize it would be a mistake to split up the children. Morganne would want me to keep them together in the home we created for them. I must try to make them happy.

Reluctantly I tell Mum, "I'm sorry I made the suggestion. I've changed my mind."

She turns on me, looking grim. "You wicked man. You've been very deceitful!"

Dad doesn't say much. But he privately continues to urge Mum to join him in Stamford at the parsonage. She has to accept my decision.

She helps me interview over a dozen candidates for her replacement. None of them seems acceptable to her. As time goes by, I feel more and more determined to be independent. We find a housekeeper who, we both agree, seems capable. She will move into the house with her ten-year-old son. I have no idea what to expect.

At first the new arrangements seem to work well with Mum's living in Stamford. She comes over to help the housekeeper with the ironing while Dad takes Debby for a ride in the stroller. I still drive the car pool and drop Davy off at Greenwich Country Day on the way to the train station. The housekeeper drives Chris to Round Hill Nursery School and takes care of Debby. At night she holds dinner until I return. I sing a favorite vesper from my childhood and stay with them until they fall asleep. A few hours later, I take them to the bathroom. Sometimes they wet the bed and wake up crying. I become more and more exhausted.

Completely strung-out, I fall asleep at work with my head on my desk. Even my work on pensions loses its fascination. I wander around the office in a daze vaguely realizing I could be fired. Morganne is not there to encourage me or say, "Now, David Ball, listen to me!" At lunchtime I drift across the street to the Yale Club. On the fifth floor and hidden in the back of the library waits a large room with a piano where I can listen to recordings. I usually have the room to myself. I close the door, slump in a beat-up leather chair, and play a scratchy record by the Wiffenpoofs. "We're little black sheep who have gone astray, baa baa baa."

I brood over the course of my life since wartime England. Moody gave me the opportunity to come to America, which rose to meet my expectations of the Promised Land. A scholarship to Yale and election to Skull and Bones made everything seem possible. My good fortune continued at Columbia when I met Morganne, who shared my dream of making the world a better place and helped me practice what I preached. I found a top job with a Wall Street law firm and even served on the Mayor's Task Force on Tax Policy. But I haven't made much of a difference, and I'm certainly not helping to run the country. Worst of all, I've lost my glimmering girl and the mother of my children. My house has come crashing down. I'm a failure.

The only person who seems to understand is Dad. Instead of criticism, he offers reassurance. "All things work together for good to them who love God." What an incredible promise! I don't know how it could be true in this terrible time, but I hang on to it like a lifeline, day in and day out.

In February the housekeeper threatens to quit if she has to work at night. This means I can't socialize unless I find another babysitter. She arrives in the morning just in time to take over before I head for the office and leaves the moment I return. On the edge of collapse, I grab something to eat, tidy the playroom, and put the kids to bed. However, I decide to persevere with her. I remember the series of babysitters in Morganne's childhood, and I don't want to do that to her children.

Christopher sometimes has nightmares. I tell him to get in bed with me until he goes to sleep, and then I carry him back to his room. When we drive in the car he lays his head on my lap.

Debby's blond hair and sweet smile remind me of Morganne. She was only one when her mother died. I feel sure she won't experience the same loss as her brothers.

Davy remembers his confrontations with Morganne and asks, "Why did she act that way? What did I do? Why did she leave?" I don't know how to answer. He finds it hard to concentrate on his schoolwork. His teacher at Greenwich Country Day says he has learning disabilities and suggests he repeat first grade. She also makes clear her preference for me to find another school.

As I become more and more exhausted, I realize beyond a shadow of a doubt I can never give my children the warmth and affection they need while I remain so traumatized and lonely myself. I need a new wife who will also be a mother to them. I pray, "Lord, help me find the right person."

# Chapter Fifteen

## *Beginning Again*

Mum says, "David, I wish you'd come to our church. There's a young widow I want you to meet." She's still trying to reel me in. I'm curious, but I don't want Mum picking my next partner.

I start to accept invitations to dinner from sympathetic neighbors. Everyone encourages me to consider dating again. But I think to myself, "Who's going to be willing to take on three small children?" Many of the single women in Greenwich are divorced and already have children of their own.

On the way to the train station a year and a half after Morganne's death, I run into my friend Alex Ercklentz, who was a year ahead of me at Yale. He exudes confidence as partner at Brown Brothers Harriman, a private bank on Wall Street famous for its connection with Averell Harriman and his family. Alex reaches out his hand. "How are you doing?"

"I'm fine," I reply, but add with trepidation, "please don't hesitate to introduce me to anyone you think might be suitable."

"I know just the person for you," he announces.

"Who's that?"

"My secretary, Carol Gore."

"Would she be interested in taking on three small children?" I ask skeptically.

"Yes, she would."

I wonder how he could possibly know, but he sweeps on, quite sure of himself. "At Brown Brothers it's a tradition to take your secretary to lunch on her birthday. Why don't you join us on Carol's birthday, December twenty-first?"

When I arrive at the Lunch Club, Alex has also invited another business friend, so there are four of us. Carol, with her long brown hair, sparkling blue-green eyes, and a lively personality, attracts all of my attention. I discover she graduated in 1972 from the College of William and Mary. In 1970, she took time off from college to live with her family when her father was stationed with the navy in Hong Kong.

To my astonishment, Carol adds, "I've been accepted at Harvard Business School, but I've deferred enrollment in order to get more work experience on Wall Street. Two nights a week I am taking graduate courses in accounting and finance at New York University."

I tell her about my job at Babcock & Wilcox and my interest in pensions. She smiles as she listens to my story about growing up in England and my description of the children. Today is her twenty-third birthday and I'm thirty-six, but we seem to have a lot to talk about.

A few days later, I pluck up the courage to call her on the phone. "Are you free to go out on Saturday?"

She quickly replies, "No."

"How about Sunday?"

"No," she repeats flatly.

In desperation, I ask, "Well, how about the following weekend?"

After a moment's silence, she bursts out, "Excuse me, but aren't you married?"

"No, I'm a widower."

She says, "Oh! In that case I'm free for lunch on Sunday."

Carol lives in a fifth-floor walkup in an old brownstone on Eighty-Fifth Street. Full of enthusiasm, I leap up the stairs two at a time. She hears me coming and greets me at the top with a giggle. "You passed the first test! My roommate and I agree that any man who has trouble making the stairs is not a contender."

This sounds encouraging.

She offers a simple lunch of tomato soup and some special freshly baked rolls. She explains, "I really enjoyed our conversation, but you talked about your children, and I assumed you were married. I didn't realize your wife had died. I'm so sorry."

We banter through a leisurely afternoon of paintings at the Frick Collection on Fifth Avenue. With pretended seriousness we speculate about an oil painting by Fragonard depicting a courtly lover handing some letters to his lady. Could such a formal encounter promise a more passionate relationship? We linger for a spaghetti dinner on Lexington Avenue. I have a sense of warmth and healing. When I take her home at ten o'clock, I know I'd like to see her again.

The following weekend I pick up Carol for dinner. Women wear really short skirts these days, and she slips into the shortest, most distracting dress I've ever seen. How lucky can I get? My hair is getting thin on top!

She sits close to me in a French restaurant and orders a glass of Chablis. I propose a toast to Fragonard.

Warmed by the wine, I inquire, "How did you like Hong Kong?"

"I found it fascinating," she replies. "During the Vietnam War mainland China was closed to Americans. My father speaks Mandarin Chinese and his job included intelligence. He and my mother held elegant dinner parties in our apartment halfway up The Peak. Our guests consisted of many British and international people, including members of the Chinese establishment in Hong Kong who liked to drop tidbits of news about the mainland to my father, to hedge their bets in case of a Communist takeover. My mother often needed me to fill a place at the table."

"What made you come to New York?"

"I love big cities. On my way back from Hong Kong, I spent some time in London and attended summer school at the University of Paris at the Sorbonne."

"How did you end up at Brown Brothers?"

She takes another sip of Chablis. "I took the best job I could find in the six weeks before my money ran out. I had looked for a job as a management trainee, but as a French major from a Southern college, without an executive wardrobe, I couldn't find any position except as a secretary. The only clothes I had were the ones I made myself."

I glance at her dress and her long, sexy legs. They look fine to me. I take a large swig of wine.

A few weeks later we try skiing at Stratton Mountain in Vermont. All goes well as I help her on the beginner slopes. At the end of the weekend on the way home, disaster strikes. The car breaks down. I'm mortified, but Carol says cheerfully, "This is our first taste of adversity together."

I think, *She's still interested. What a relief.* While we look for a rental car in Brattleboro, I want to level with her. I say, "There's something I want to explain before we go any further in our relationship. Morganne was depressed and committed suicide."

Carol gives me a warm smile. "I already knew that because Alex told me and I'm sorry. It must have been horrible for you." After a pause, she adds, "Why don't we include the children on our next ski trip?"

Two weeks later I meet her at the Greenwich train station with Debby sitting by my side in the front seat of the car. I move Debby to the back with the boys to make room for Carol. Perhaps this is a mistake. Debby stands defiantly in the back without a seat belt and says, "I don't like her."

Concerned about this unexpected reaction, I protest, "You don't know her yet. I'm sure you'll like her when you do."

As I drive to Stratton, the boys take turns braiding Carol's long hair. After watching for a while, Debby says, "I want a turn," and her brothers reluctantly move over. Once we arrive, Carol gets down on her hands and knees to give them horseback rides. In the morning, we enroll Davy and Chris in ski lessons and Debby in a playgroup, while Carol and I try the slopes again.

Debby seems pleased when Carol buys three black-and-white teddy bears with the smallest bear for her. But Chris says, "It could be a trick." His heart pines for Morganne.

Carol seems determined to overcome every obstacle and organizes activities, like a trip to the Bronx Zoo. The kids marvel at the enormous dinosaurs in the American Museum of Natural History and the stars moving in the night sky at the planetarium. Weekends become fun. After a safari through the lions, zebras, and giraffes at Jungle World in New Jersey, Davy asks, "Where are we going next?"

We all drive over to visit Mum and Dad in Stamford. I want their approval, although Mum, who usually is never at a loss for words, doesn't say much. Dad appears hopeful. He takes a photo of us with the children. Thank goodness for his support and encouragement!

Carol invites me to meet her own parents at their home, a farmhouse on a military base near Philadelphia. As I enter her world, I worry about their reaction to an older man whose wife committed suicide. But the brisk salute from the sentry at the gate acts like a tonic.

Carol's father, Captain Frederick Gore, commander of the Willow Grove Naval Air Station, plans to attend law school after he retires from the navy. He says, "I've been accepted at American University and William and Mary. Which would you recommend?"

"If it were me," I reply, "I would go to William and Mary."

His wife, Roie, suggests bringing the children down for an air show by the Blue Angels. Brilliant! I quickly accept her invitation. On the big day, after a breathtaking performance, Captain Gore arranges to have the boys photographed with the daredevil pilots.

Carol and I take a trip to Williamsburg with her college roommate and her roommate's boyfriend. To my astonishment, as we walk into the lobby of the Williamsburg Inn, we run into Morganne's godmother, Blanche. I say, "Oh my goodness!" and for a moment I don't know what to expect.

Blanche responds cheerfully, "I'm so pleased to meet Carol." I realize I don't need to worry about her approval.

Her warm greeting encourages me to consider the next step. Over the last two months my life has become entwined with Carol's. We have a lot in common, starting with the Episcopal church. She has traveled widely as a navy junior, and we share an interest in business and politics. I admire her competence and trust her judgment, to say nothing about her good looks and long, sexy legs. She would make a good mother and she understands the necessity of living on a budget. I feel ready to take a leap of faith and hope that our relationship will continue to grow. I pray, "Lord, Carol looks like the one. Please help her make the right decision!"

On a sunny winter day, we meet for lunch in Battery Park at the tip of Manhattan. Carol wears red high-heel shoes and brims with self-confidence. I know the moment is propitious. I ask, "Will you marry me?"

"Maybe!" she replies. "I'd like some time to think it over."

A few days later she tells me she's made a list of pros and cons.

I ask humbly, "What are they?"

"The biggest arguments against are that I'll be giving up Harvard and the possibility of a business career."

I realize with all her talent, this is a lot for her to let go, and inquire, "What are the arguments in favor?"

"I'm in love with you. Sometimes I feel certain you're the man that I'm destined to marry."

"Anything else?" I ask.

She smiles. "I feel compassion for the children. They're little lost souls starving for love and attention. I know you'd be a good provider, so I'd be able to stay home and concentrate on their needs."

Two weeks pass in suspense. Then one evening she hands me a letter addressed to Harvard Business School. It says, "I have decided to give up my place because I have been offered a more challenging opportunity."

What a miracle! She wants me. I hold her close and say a quiet prayer of thanks. I was afraid of being rejected again.

Mum rallies at the news and offers to give a bridal shower. When Carol arrives at the parsonage in Stamford, she finds the living room full of ladies from the church. Mum hands out pieces of paper containing verses from love stories in the Bible. Each person must identify the relevant story. Carol is not as familiar as they are with the Bible and has no idea what to say. But she appreciates their gifts of kitchen utensils, dishtowels, and a can opener.

Even though Mum would prefer someone from her own church, she welcomes Carol as a mother for my children. With revived feelings of warmth, I want to show my appreciation for all she has done. I scrape together enough money for a new upright piano. She wants one for church meetings at home after leaving her old piano behind in Attica.

Since my brother Jonathan has gone as a missionary to Japan, I ask Stuart Lovejoy, my friend from St. Barnabas, to serve as best man. We check into a motel a mile away from the main entrance to the Willow Grove Naval Air Station. Unbelievably, Stuart drives off to the rehearsal at the chapel on the base forgetting that I need a ride. As I struggle to knot my tie and head for the base on foot, I shiver with twinges of fear. Why would anyone so perfect want to marry me? I'm damaged goods. Carol might change her mind.

The rehearsal is already underway when I reach the door of the chapel. I spot her standing in the distance in front of the altar. She looks stunningly beautiful in an orange and pink dress that I haven't seen before. Once she sees me in the doorway, she lights up with joy. Her radiant smile tells me all I need to know.

We marry on July 28, 1973, a blazing hot day. Dad helps conduct the service. Mum, whose dress sense is usually zero, looks lovely in a green outfit that Carol's mother helped her find. The bridal party includes David Holbrook, Bob Giegengack, and Carol's sisters, Beth and Anne. My loyal roommate Nick Kangas and his wife, Sandy, drive all the way out from Chicago. A supporting band of Skull and Bones friends seems to promise better days ahead.

Carol, steady and self-assured, takes my arm. David Holbrook says to me, laughing, "You look ebullient!"

Although full of high spirits at the reception, I worry about the children. I realize, too late, that although they've known Carol for six months, I haven't prepared them sufficiently for this big moment in their lives. Davy, age eight, wanders around like a clown, wearing a hat belonging to one of the bridesmaids. Chris, age five, tickles Carol with a feather to see if she will sneeze. Debby, age three, seems confused and clings to Mum.

*David and Carol with Christopher, Debby, and Dave,*
*at Willow Grove Naval Air Station in 1973.*

Mum and Dad take care of them while Carol and I go on our honeymoon to Little Dix Bay on British Virgin Gorda. I know the children will feel safe while we're away, and I want to help them understand better when we return. In a way, we take them with us. When Carol unpacks, I find the books she's brought for honeymoon reading are on child psychology.

We start our new life together with hope and joy. We laugh with delight as she teaches me to dance for the first time in a natural way to the fast beat of Bob Marley's music. By the grace of God and with Carol's help, I've been rescued from the brink of despair. I have a chance to begin again.

# Chapter Sixteen

## *The Perils of a New Job*

Carol says, "I want a home that we choose together. I can't live in a place with so many memories of your first marriage." So we move to a house on Orchard Hill Lane in Glenville, a different part of Greenwich.

She takes over with aplomb. After discovering I haven't claimed reimbursement for medical expenses, she starts filing the insurance forms. She wants to buy a Singer sewing machine so she can make and repair the children's clothes. On Saturday mornings she encourages them to crowd into our brand-new, king-size bed for a cuddle. At dinnertime we take turns reading them stories from an illustrated children's Bible.

Although she studies books about child development from the Greenwich library, Carol can't find anything about stepfamilies. We both believe with love we will overcome the problems. We don't know it's unrealistic to expect a stepmother to take the place of a natural mother. Each day as I leave for work, I trust her to take good care of the kids. I don't need to worry about them anymore.

I tell the children about the special rolls that Carol produced on our first date. "They made me want to marry her."

Eight-year-old Davy picks up on the remark and pleads, "Please make us some marriage rolls."

She beams. "Of course I will."

He puts his arms around her. "Thanks, Mom!"

I glance at Carol in her short shorts with her long, sexy legs. She's barely old enough to be his natural mother. But when I mention this, she says laughing, "It would be possible!" She wants to make it official, so one day we take the children before a judge and Carol adopts them as her own.

We transfer the boys to public elementary school in Glenville and send Debby to nursery school. Davy wants me to help him learn to read. His favorite book is *Go Dog Go*.

The book gives Carol an idea. With the help of the children, she finds a wire-haired fox terrier puppy. Davy calls the puppy Choo Choo because she dashes around like a little train, and that becomes her family name.

On Christmas Eve, Carol encourages the kids to leave a glass of milk and a cookie for Santa, and a carrot for his reindeer. Davy pours the milk and enthusiastically picks out a carrot. After a rocky relationship with Morganne, he wants to believe in his new mom. We start calling him Dave.

Carol gives me a record by the Carpenters with a song titled "Top of the World." She says, "That's how I feel." The warmth of her love has transformed my life. She has created order out of chaos, and we all seem to be enacting the spirit of *Go Dog Go*.

An unsolicited letter from a headhunter gives me a further chance to get going. The headhunter says an unidentified client needs a corporate secretary. I show it to Carol at bedtime, remarking in jest, "I enjoyed this position at Southeastern Public Service Corporation. Maybe I should look into it."

She studies the letter carefully before she replies, "I think you should."

In April 1974, after many interviews, I become assistant secretary of AMAX Inc., a metals and mining firm and one of the two hundred largest industrial companies in the United States. With the corporate headquarters sharing the same building as Radio City Music Hall in Rockefeller Center, it seems like a glamorous opportunity. The chairman is a Scotsman named Ian MacGregor who came to America to purchase metal for tanks for the British government during World War II. I take an instant liking to this brilliant, soft-spoken Scot, and he seems to like me.

In July the board elects me secretary. Some of the directors, like former Undersecretary of State George Ball, have served in the government. I sit quietly at my place next to the chairman while he describes his participation in an economic summit with President Ford. I feel privileged to have a place at the table.

My new boss wants to list the common stock of AMAX on all the major stock exchanges so I prepare listing applications for London, Amsterdam, Brussels, Paris, Frankfurt, Vienna, Zurich, Geneva, and Tokyo. Carol jumps at the chance to fly with me to Tokyo for the listing ceremony, while my parents take care of the children. When she was three years old, she lived in Tokyo. Her father, who speaks Mandarin Chinese, translated at the truce talks in Panmunjom to end the Korean War. He left his wife and two girls in the home of a Christian professor at Tokyo University named Dr. Kagawa.

After a trip on the bullet train to Kyoto, the ancient capital of Japan, we find a Japanese family in brilliantly colored ceremonial costume waiting for us near the entrance of the Okura hotel. The head of AMAX Japan has found Mrs. Kagawa. She claims to recognize Carol, whom she last saw at age three. We all laugh when she says, "You haven't changed!"

We invite them inside for refreshments. Mrs. Kagawa entertains us with a classical Japanese instrument with three strings called a samisen. She sings a haunting melody. I ask, "What do the words mean?"

She translates, "Time flies like an arrow, young people, so make good use of your time."

The arrow of the refrain grazes me. I think again about Martin Luther King Jr. He died younger than I am now. His time on earth was short, but he made good use of it. I still want to make the world a better place, but my arrow has gotten wedged in the bullet train of an engrossing career. I must find space to reflect on where it is taking me.

Back in America, I delay soul searching. I'm too caught up in using my time to help Ian MacGegor run AMAX. After he decides to move the corporate headquarters to Greenwich, I begin to drop by his office first thing in the morning to chat. On one such occasion, to my delight, he brings up pensions. He says, "With record earnings, it's time for a cost-of-living increase under the Salaried Retirement Plan. Put it on the agenda for the next board meeting."

As I become more involved at AMAX, Carol becomes exhausted taking care of her three rambunctious stepchildren. She looks for escape in romantic novels about ladies of quality. She sighs. "Sometimes I dream about my carefree life in Hong Kong, driving my TR 3 sports car down to the beach at Repulse Bay."

The pressure builds. She loses weight and has trouble getting to sleep. Finally, she explodes, "You aren't interested in family activities or romantic outings anymore. We should go to a marriage counselor."

Not wanting to admit we have a problem, I reply, "We ought to be able to work it out ourselves."

Her doctor suggests getting away for a weekend at least once a month, but it is difficult to follow his advice. Under Dave's leadership, the children specialize in sabotaging babysitters. We feel grateful if they spend the weekend with Mum and Dad. Debby, whom Mum calls "my little angel," wakes up early and climbs in bed with Grandma while Grandpa fetches a cup of tea. At night Grandma entertains them with Bible stories. She spends a lot of time brushing Debby's hair. She asks a lot of questions. "What time do you usually go to bed?" "Does your mother hear you say your prayers?" "Does she tell you about Jesus?"

I don't mind Mum's talking about the Lord. I assume she will have a positive influence. After all, I want to pass on my faith to my children. But her preoccupation with Debby annoys Carol, who thinks the boys resent it.

One of our greatest challenges is my unfinished grief work. Ever since Morganne died, I have avoided driving over the Tappan Zee Bridge. Carol says, "You need to put it behind you. Next time we visit our friends in New Jersey we should go that way." When I reluctantly follow her suggestion, I glance uneasily at the railing and the river swirling below. As I try to repress my horror, I think, *This bridge never will be easy.* My stomach churns all evening, but at night when I go to sleep with the reassuring comfort of Carol's arm around me, the terror fades away.

Since Carol is an Episcopalian, she fits right in at St. Barnabas. On an overcast winter day we sit in the front pew as usual so the children can participate in the service. Suddenly, an African American lady rushes forward. I vaguely remember Morganne once complimented this woman on her paintings in an art show at the church. Breathing hard and sweating profusely, she starts talking to the congregation during the opening hymn. I suddenly realize she is accusing me of Morganne's death.

I try to sing but swallow hard. The words blur in front of my eyes. Carol moves close to me and shares my hymnbook. Thank goodness for her loyalty, but I wonder what the children think, and behind us the congregation listens.

Two of the ushers come to lead the woman away. After the service the rector says, "She's not in good mental health and has just been released from a hospital in the city." I hurry back to the car with my eyes locked on the cold gray flagstones.

With Morganne's suicide hanging over our lives, how can I concentrate on anything other than my family and my job? I feel Dr. King's inspiration slipping farther away. It's unrealistic to think about politics or trying to make a difference in social issues.

Another disturbing problem begins to emerge. Carol says, "I feel as if I'm living with the ghost of your first wife. Sometimes I think you only married me so I would take care of your children."

I try to explain. "I loved you when I married you, and I love you even more today. But I can't obliterate my years with Morganne."

Carol shakes her head.

I don't discuss Morganne with the children for fear of undermining their relationship with their stepmother. I don't speak of her at all. We don't even have a photograph on display. It's as if Morganne had never lived. I want to protect my marriage and make it work. However, this leaves me with a big aching hole in my life.

One day I drive over to Buckfield Lane and look back through the trees to the stream and the pond. There on top of the grassy bank sits the house that Morganne and I built, surrounded by walls of dry stone I lugged into place with the help of a wheelbarrow. My eyes mist over and I choke up. I wish I could tell Morganne about everything that has happened.

Struggling with grief, I've been only vaguely aware that the children are haunted by their own sense of loss. The traumatic bite of abandonment seems to recur again and again, like the chills and fever of malaria that have haunted Mum since her time in India. Sometimes Christopher sobs in the night. Dave's learning problems get worse. Five-year-old Debby is confused by the changes she's endured. Bewildered myself, I have no clear explanation to give her.

Carol meets my brother, Jonathan, and his family for the first time when they return from Japan. After floundering with the language for two years, he ended up as house parent for twenty teenage children of fellow missionaries. This was not exactly what he had expected. A year later, frustrated with the children and the language, he decided to come back. He finds a position at Twin Valley Bible Church in the Amish country of Pennsylvania.

Mum is not fazed. She says, "He should have his own church one day."

The Evangelical Congregational Church thrives under Dad's usual dedicated ministry and pastoral care. Four hundred people attend on Sundays, and the church pays off the debt on a new building. Dad says humbly, "I don't have a lot of fancy degrees, but they seem to like my preaching." At age sixty-eight he tries to retire, and for the first time since they came to America, he and Mum purchase their own home ten miles away in Ridgefield, Connecticut. They join Ridgefield Baptist Church. Behind her chair in the living room, Mum hangs the portrait of her Hadley ancestor with his top hat and hoop. I still don't understand why she gave up the life of affluence reflected in the painting.

When the pastor of the Ridgefield Baptist Church leaves, Dad is asked to step in as interim minister. After two more years he retires for good, and the church holds a party to celebrate his fifty years of ministry.

Mum has never criticized Dad's sermons. Their partnership, although suffering from her inhibitions about physical warmth, has succeeded because they feel it has helped them serve the Lord. Now, as we stand in the church parking lot after the retirement party, I ask Dad about his plans. He says with a twinkle in his eye, like a farmer returning to the land, "We've got two acres. I think I'll try a vegetable garden."

Mum retorts, "I don't mind what you do, but I'm not quitting. I'm going to serve the Lord until the day I die!" Her voice quavers as she speaks, and her hands tremble slightly. Her face is lined, and her legs are thick with varicose veins. She is seventy, and determination drives her on. I think, as I never used to, that single-mindedness costs her something. She soon finds another mission field, insisting that they start driving to a small Baptist church in Darien to help expand the work with young people.

Sometimes we go to Vermont for the weekend. After they graduate from the Little Cub Ski School, I take each of the children up the chairlift. I hold them proudly in front of me while they snowplow down the mountain for the first time. Just as Dad taught me, I teach them how to curl old newspapers into rolls and tie them in knots to build a fire. After Carol describes the Yule log ceremony at the College of William and Mary, the children insist on looking for the largest log to place on top. At night while the snow drifts past the window, they curl up in front of a roaring blaze to listen to stories about Paddington Bear. I hear them say their prayers and sing my vesper when they go to bed.

I want to share with them the exhilaration of a family gathering like that on Boxing Day at my grandfather's farm in Cheltenham, so I invite Jonathan and Ruth to bring their families to join us at Stratton for Christmas. I also invite Mum and Dad, but Mum flatly refuses to go to a "worldly" ski resort.

In a rare flash of independence, Dad decides to attend. This puts Mum on the spot. To our great surprise, at the last minute when she realizes we intend to go ahead without her, she changes her mind. She's not going to be left out of a family get-together. In fact, she enjoys organizing activities for the younger children. She laughs hysterically with the rest of us when Jonathan, who has never skied before, good-naturedly describes skidding out of control and crashing into a snow fence.

Ruth tells me the hilarity reminds her of an incident shortly after she began married life with Jim in England. Mum and Dad had taken them to a family party given by my cousin Joan, who lives in an old rectory near Chippenham on the banks of the river Avon. Mum had just had her hair done and wore her best clothes and a new pair of shoes. Jim persuaded her to go for a paddle in a canoe. He teased her by rocking the boat, but unfortunately he rocked too hard and the canoe tipped over. They both fell into the river.

The family peered anxiously over the edge of the bank anticipating a furious outburst from Mum, but to everyone's amazement she came up laughing. Once Dad saw her struggle safely to her feet, he walked along the bank taking photographs.

Mum laughed and laughed until the tears streamed down her already wet face, as she helped right the canoe and bring it back to the bank. She said, "It just tickled my funny bone."

As Ruth and I chuckle about Mum's reference to her funny bone, I realize that apart from launching those terrible guilt-laden accusations, my missionary mother is really on my side. I try to forget about the guilt trips.

In the summer Carol and I take the children to musicals at the Weston Playhouse in Vermont. On Sundays at the Weston Priory, we sing hymns with Benedictine monks, accompanied by an electric guitar. Carol likes one of their songs: "Wherever you go I will go." She says, "That song makes me think about you." I realize that, thanks to her, my shattered self-confidence is beginning to heal.

At the very moment when I begin to feel settled, she says, "I'm ready for children of my own."

# Chapter Seventeen

## *THE SUNNY BANKERS OF AMERICA*

I know Carol has waited four years before expanding our family so Dave, Chris, and Debby could feel comfortable with her. I agree the time has come. She says, "We'll need a house with another bedroom."

After looking all over town, she finds an unpretentious colonial on Round Hill Road, near St. Barnabas. It needs a lot of work. What interests me are the three small overgrown fields, a neglected stable, and a chicken house. This country place takes me back to my childhood adventures at Sunny Bank, my grandfather's smallholding in the Cotswolds. We decide to adopt the same name for our new abode. When Grandfather's widow, Auntie Gracie, hears about this, she sends us a Christmas card addressed, "From the Sunny Bankers of England to the Sunny Bankers of America."

I start the dilapidated tractor to cut the grass for the first time. Debby runs over to ask for a ride. I lift her tenderly onto my lap to share the triumph of mowing our own fields.

Carol rejoices at becoming pregnant. Mum and Dad are delighted when I tell them the news. It is Mum who rushes Carol to the hospital when her water breaks during a checkup at the doctor's office. She has a difficult labor, but early on May 11, 1978, she gives birth to a healthy boy whom we name Jonathan, which means "gift from God." Debby, who wanted a girl, tells a friend at church, "It's a boy, but it's all right!"

Carol returns from the hospital exhausted and grateful for Mum's help. When I arrive home from work, I find Carol upstairs in bed, contentedly feeding her baby. Mum, full of good cheer, bustles around the kitchen fixing dinner for the rest of us. At night she rocks Jon to sleep with a lullaby.

*Mum and Dad in Ridgefield in 1977 after David tells them Carol is pregnant.*

An unexpected visitor shows up after Mum is back in Ridgefield. He introduces himself as Lakai, the son of one of the girls she taught in the bamboo church in India fifty years ago. She tells me with satisfaction, "Lakai is a minister to the Lakhers. There aren't any missionaries there anymore, but the mission has grown to over sixty churches with thousands of members." She sets about raising money for a jeep to help Lakai visit his people.

She and Dad come to stay at Sunny Bank in August while we fly to England with the children. Dad plans to paint the house, and Mum schemes to invite my brother and his family to spend a few days enjoying our pool. As our boisterous youngsters squeeze into the car, the old folks stand at the back door laughing. Mum calls out, "Give everybody our love."

With her usual self-confidence, Carol breast-feeds Jon while watching the changing of the guard at Buckingham Palace. We drive to Gloucester Cathedral, where the kids rub some brasses of early saints. At Kington Mead Farm I leap at the chance to help bale wheat with my cousin Roger, just as my father did with Uncle Gerald when I was a boy.

We visit my cousin John, who has just left a job raising pheasants for the queen at Great Windsor Park to become gamekeeper on an estate in Hampshire. His wife wakes me early in the morning with a call from Dad. He is at Stamford hospital.

He says, "Mum had a stroke while driving home from a Sunday school teachers' meeting in Darien. She crashed your car as she pulled off the road."

Standing by the bedroom door in my pajamas, I shiver in a cold draft. I pray for Mum, but she seems far away.

A few hours later Dad calls again. Stunned, I hear his voice break on the words, "Mum has died." I'm too dazed for the moment to figure out what it means. Dad seems crushed. A dark cloud descends. I want to get home to comfort him.

I offer instantly, "Come and live with us."

Later my heart aches to learn that Dad returns to our house from the hospital alone. He doesn't want to wake Jonathan and Arlene in Pennsylvania, so he sits in the kitchen and waits until morning before he calls them. His mother died when he was eleven, and now the strong capable wife, who always told him what to do, has gone. He cries. He's a motherless child again.

Debby sobs at the funeral, telling everyone, "Grandma loved me!" She stays upset for a long time. Dave and Chris remain silent, as if the brutal trauma of their mother's suicide has left them indifferent to another death.

We bury Mum in Putnam Cemetery in Greenwich, not far from Morganne. I remember with gratitude how, despite her great disappointment over my not becoming a minister, she dropped everything to help me when Morganne died. I desperately needed her during those first terrible months. I remember the hug she gave me when she walked into the house on Buckfield Lane after driving down from Attica. It seemed so unusual and so appropriate. It took the earthquake of a suicide to shake loose her feelings so she could show physical affection.

Strangely enough, I feel sad, but I don't cry. I cried for weeks after Morganne's death, but expressing emotion was natural in our warm, loving relationship. With Mum, I learned to repress my feelings. Ruth has the same reaction. She feels an enormous shock, but sheds no tears. She says, "I can imagine Mum doing anything except dying."

Mum never stopped trying to take charge of her world. Her way of maintaining control was to insist something was God's will. Ruth and I agree that Mum was sincere in believing she unerringly knew God's will. If we didn't comply with her wishes, she lashed out with guilt-inducing accusations. She didn't consider other points of view. Ruth says, "Even when she told Dad to take the wrong turn in the car, she never said she was sorry when it turned out to be a mistake. It takes a sense of self-worth to admit that one is wrong and apologize. Deep down she must have been coping with insecurity."

I wonder if I will ever know what made her so vulnerable. Something catastrophic must have happened. I wish I had shown more interest in her past while she was alive. She seemed closer after our baby was born but now she has gone.

Jonathan hears the deacons of Ebenezer Bible Chapel, near Morgantown, Pennsylvania, have unanimously recommended calling him as pastor. He says, "Mum believed it was the Lord's will for me to go to Ebenezer," and accepts. Dad sells his place in Ridgefield and moves in with us. We enclose a screened porch and create a little apartment for him at the back of the house. He continues to minister in Darien, just as Mum would wish.

While he sorts out his possessions, Dad finds the portrait of my Hadley ancestor, the little boy with red-brown hair who is supposed to look like Mum. I hang it behind my black leather chair in the library, pausing to look into his face. He seems different now from the wealthy ancestor I used to imagine. Despite his top hat and hoop, he has the innocent face of a child. Mum never explained who he was. Come to think of it, she didn't tell us much about her own childhood either.

Although we seldom mention Morganne, we are still haunted by her death. When Debby starts school, she asks, "What shall I tell the children at school about my mother who died?"

I don't know what to say, but Carol replies sympathetically, "You don't have to tell them anything if you don't want to. Just say she got sick and died."

The boys never talk about Morganne, but once in a while I still hear Christopher crying in the night. Sometimes he crawls into bed with Dave or comes looking for me in his sleep.

Dad helps renovate the chicken house for six Rhode Island Red chickens and a big, strutting, fierce-looking rooster, which we call Lord Sunny Bank. Our neighbor complains about Lord Sunny Bank crowing early in the morning so we install room-darkening shades to delay his wake-up call. Dad chuckles. "This is posh compared with our homemade fowl house in Gloucester!"

His enthusiasm for the land is infectious. He suggests we invite our neighbor to pasture his pony in one of our fields. Several months later a friend gives us a retired polo pony named Critter, and we buy another horse for a few hundred dollars. In November we work outside together in a fine-misty drizzle, opening up a box stall for the horses. Dad says, "This is a real English farm day! Many times as a boy I worked outside in the rain." As he heaves bales of hay down from the loft with the vigor of a young farmhand, he looks as if he'll live forever.

My job requires several trips to Paris to work on the listing of the common stock on the Paris Bourse, or stock exchange. Unfortunately, the minister of finance blocks the listing. This results in a long delay. I ask Pierre Gousseland, a Frenchman who is head of AMAX Molybdenum, to intercede at the ministry. Later he tells me of his surprise at seeing written on the listing application, "Non. Valéry Giscard d'Estaing." We laugh at overcoming such a formidable obstacle—a finance minister who eventually becomes president of France.

To my delight, my boss Ian MacGregor tells me to take charge of preparing the proxy statement and form 10K. He also arranges for my election as a vice president of AMAX. I love attending board meetings, getting to know the directors, and listening to their private deliberations. In fact, I tell Carol, "I enjoy this job so much, I'd almost do it for nothing."

*David holding Jonathan, with Christopher, Deborah, Dave holding Choo Choo, and Carol at Sunny Bank in 1979.*

My serenity is rattled when the board approves the sale of 20 percent of AMAX stock to Socal, a big oil concern. I can't help wondering what will happen if they try to take over the company. Will I lose my job? Even more unnerving, my mentor Ian MacGregor retires to become a partner of Lehman Brothers. This leaves me in the lurch. To survive I need to build a relationship with Pierre Gousseland, now the new chief executive.

The worst shock of all comes when my assistant rushes into my office with a story on the front page of *The Wall Street Journal.* It says, "Mystery Phone Call on Takeover Offer Picked Up on Radio." Someone identified as "Mr. Eavesdrop" has picked up a phone conversation on a car telephone by Pierre. He discussed calling a special board meeting to consider a takeover proposal by Socal. The article raises questions about proper consideration of the proposal.

I feel sick. Pierre was talking to me.

I fear the story in the *Journal* will undermine my relationship with my new boss. The Securities and Exchange Commission opens an investigation. But when we discuss it, Pierre doesn't seem upset. He explains to the SEC that the article misreported what happened. He had called me about canceling a dinner invitation to someone who was a candidate for membership on the board, but not yet a director.

The incident disappears like a rogue gust of wind, and I relax. The price of molybdenum soars upward, like a kite, and the takeover proposal flies away beyond Socal's grasp. Pierre treats me to lunch at La Crémaillère in Greenwich. As he sips a glass of Pineau de Charantes, he asks mischievously, "Whatever happened to Mr. Eavesdrop?"

Life is more peaceful at home. In his quiet way, Dad has a profound impact on all of us. One evening when I rush into his apartment after work, I find him kneeling by the side of his bed. He is a godly man like Martin Luther King Jr. He makes me feel loved.

On Saturday mornings he invites Chris and Debby for a special treat of boiled eggs, toast, marmalade, and tea. Afternoons he takes baby Jon in the stroller to explore back-country lanes. When Dave starts seventh grade, Dad drives the car pool. They all seem to think of him as a guardian angel. I no longer hear them crying in the middle of the night.

As he emerges from Mum's shadow, he sometimes comes to St. Barnabas with us instead of worshiping in Darien. On seeing him sitting next to me in the pew, one of my friends jokes, "Nice to see your brother in church with you!" Carol and the children laugh. How amazing! Mum would never come near the place. But by joining us, Dad gives us great joy.

Carol and I teach Sunday school, making sure the class always includes one of our children. On Christmas Eve, Dave helps the participants memorize their parts for the church pageant. Chris sparkles as a narrator, and Debby shines as an angel. In January 1980, after many years as parish clerk, the vestry elects me senior warden.

During summer nights, the sound of the horses chomping on the grass outside our bedroom window conjures up memories of the cattle grazing in home field at Uncle Gerald's Kington Mead Farm. Every morning the horses stand near the gate waiting for me to take their oats to a wooden trough. I fill the water bucket and carry a bale of hay out to the middle of the field, where they paw the flakes of hay apart while I feed the chickens and the barn cats. I remember that once, like Dad, I wanted to be a farmer. Now I feel like one.

I ask Carol, "How would you like to own a farm in England?"

"It's not practical," she replies. "We wouldn't get to use it very often."

Reluctantly, I agree she is right. However, in the back of my mind I cultivate a dream of owning a farm.

Dad must be dreaming too. One Sunday morning after church in Darien, he says, "Several of the single ladies have invited me to dinner."

Carol gives me a knowing look.

I ask, "Why don't you accept?"

"Oh, no," he replies. "It would give the wrong impression."

I overlook the conversation, assuming he enjoys living with us. It doesn't occur to me he misses a strong partner.

A few weeks later he takes me by surprise. "I'm thinking of getting married."

"To whom?" I gasp.

"I'm not going to tell you because she hasn't accepted yet."

"Is it someone at Darien Baptist Church?"

"It could be someone in England or America."

Carol and I speculate it might be the lady who plays the organ at Darien. We don't realize how much we would miss his warm, cheerful presence.

Speculation at home is matched by excitement at work. Pierre Gousseland tells me to expect a call from the Secret Service. President Ford has agreed to join the AMAX board. What an honor! The agent advises me to address our new member as Mr. President or President Ford, and I pass on the information to the directors.

On his first day he sits at the table puffing on his pipe waiting for the meeting to start. Knowing he graduated from Yale Law School in 1941, I try to imagine what the university was like in those days. He must have studied in the same library where I wrote my paper on how to defeat pupil placement laws.

*David with President Gerald Ford after an AMAX board meeting in New York in 1982. (Courtesy of Bruce Ando).*

The research paper brings an unexpected dividend when an African American lawyer named Bill Coleman becomes a director. After graduating from Harvard Law School, Coleman clerked for Felix Frankfurter. He was the first black person to clerk for a justice of the Supreme Court. In the Ford administration he served as secretary of transportation. Now a partner in the law firm of O'Melveny & Meyers, he also serves as chairman of the NAACP Legal Defense Fund.

When I tell Bill Coleman about my research into pupil placement laws, he exclaims, "I'd love to see your paper. I worked on the brief in *Brown v. Board of Education*." Surprised and pleased, I send him a copy.

The following month as he returns the paper, he asks, "What made you interested in such an important question?"

I reply, "It all started when Martin Luther King Jr. was my guest at Yale."

He beams. "Martin Luther King Jr.? I helped him get out of jail in Georgia."

Bill Coleman's unexpected remark gives me joy. It seems as if my old hero has reentered my life. I have found a new mentor, and I look forward to working with him. I solicit his advice in drafting an amendment to the AMAX pension plan. He says, "Improving pensions is a good way to help people." His words give me a jolt. What has happened to my ideals? Is it enough to serve as senior warden at St. Barnabas?

Another benefit of my new friendship is that Bill Coleman introduces me to his partner Mike Masin. Mike and his wife Joanne invite Carol and me to spend a weekend with them at their home in Great Falls, Virginia. We drive through gently rolling hills where cattle graze in fields lined with stone walls. The countryside reminds me of Gloucestershire. I didn't know a place like this existed in America. Barely able to contain my excitement, I savor dinner in Middleburg at an old tavern called the Red Fox. With the light from a roaring fire flickering on our wine glasses, I ask Carol, "How about a farm in Virginia?"

She smiles. "That would make more sense." She was born nearby in Warrenton, and her parents live in Williamsburg.

The four of us raise our glasses to a future farm in Virginia.

I hear no more about Dad's marriage proposal until early in 1981 when I stop by his apartment after work. He sits at a small table with his favorite view of the horses in the back field. An envelope with English postage stamps lies on the table.

He says dejectedly, "She turned me down."

"Who?" I sputter in surprise.

"Sylvia Lawrence."

"Sylvia Lawrence who used to live near us on Finlay Road?"

"Yes. She's a widow. I admired her long before I met your mother. We played doubles tennis, but she was always on the wrong side of the net."

Flabbergasted, I sit down with him at the table with my head spinning. All those years when we lived almost next door on Finlay Road, I had no idea that Dad once had a romantic interest in Sylvia.

After a long pause, I ask, "Did she give you any encouragement?"

"Mum and I always called on her when we went back to England. I've continued. She's written some friendly letters."

He looks out the window at the horses nuzzling by the fence. "I asked her whether she ever thought of taking a partner. She said she has a lot of lady friends, although sometimes she misses male companionship."

"That sounds encouraging."

He continues to stare at the horses. "We exchanged letters about our personal habits and our shortcomings. My letter was about five pages long."

"That's just like you to tell her your *shortcomings*," I reply, laughing. "Why did she turn you down?"

He swings round to look soberly at me. "She's gotten used to living alone. She nursed her husband and her mother-in-law through their last illnesses. Obviously, she doesn't want to risk that again."

I exclaim with relief, "I feel very sorry for you, Dad, but I'm glad we're not going to lose you."

Dad replies, "God's will be done!"

My momentary peace of mind is soon disturbed by a startling development at AMAX, Pierre Gousseland calls me at home. "David, I don't want to spoil your evening, but I would like to call a board meeting for 2:00 p.m. Wednesday, at the request of Socal."

I remember how my career at Southeastern ended with a takeover. Uncertainty begins to gnaw in my stomach.

# Chapter Eighteen

## *A Startling Reminder of Martin Luther King*

In March 1981 I nervously listen as the board debates a formal takeover proposal from Socal. With the Socal directors absent, it votes unanimously "not to support that offer." Bill Coleman confides, "We're expecting something better."

The antitrust division of the Justice Department announces investigations into three major deals this week. They question the Socal attempt to acquire AMAX, as well as an unfriendly attempt by Seagram to take over St. Joe Minerals and a proposal by Standard Oil of Ohio to merge with Kennecot Copper. Although the stock market has natural-resource fever, with high trading volume and enormous price increases in mining stocks, Socal fails to raise its bid. As time goes by, we realize they have given up.

Some shareholders blame management for missing an opportunity, but I can't help thinking, *Thank goodness. It's back to corporate housekeeping. I have time to learn more about the portability problem with the retirement plan.*

Soon I get caught up in plans to attend Auntie Vera and Uncle Gerald's fiftieth wedding anniversary. Dad goes over to England in advance without disclosing his intentions. It turns out he hopes to see Sylvia. She had told him she would be away on a caravan trip, but when he calls from Heathrow he discovers her at home. He drives straight to Gloucester to urge her to reconsider his proposal. Although she makes no commitment, he invites her to spend the weekend in the Cotswolds with Ruth and Jim, and she accepts.

After weeks of rain, the heavens open to sun. Dad and Sylvia sit in the garden. Ruth keeps out of the way, but from the window she sees Dad pleading his cause.

The first evening, Ruth asks him privately, "How's it going?"

"Fifty-fifty," he answers. "Sylvia's afraid of the pain if I die first. I wish she felt that some happy years together would be worth it."

Dad will be seventy-four on June 26. Sylvia is sixty-eight. They both enjoy good health. The next evening Dad reports to Ruth with a grin. "She's coming around. Ninety-ten!"

Just before the time comes for Sylvia to go back to Gloucester, they walk down an old Roman road and pause at a gate. Dad says, "Sylvia, there are no obstacles to our getting married." He takes courage and kisses her.

She says, "Of course, you'll have to come live with me in Gloucester."

Ecstatically, he answers, "It will be a privilege!"

When I arrive at Ruth's house and hear the stunning news, I rejoice for Dad, but I know I will miss his company and his advice.

Forty-seven years after first feeling drawn to her, Dad marries Sylvia. After the ceremony they fly to America to spend their honeymoon with us at Sunny Bank. We purchase a convertible couch to serve as a double bed in Dad's apartment. Our boys joke about the amazing romantic Grandpa. Dave says, "With Grandma he was a lonely man, but with Sylvia he's like a kid in love."

My brother, Jonathan, suddenly resigns as pastor of Ebenezer Bible Chapel. I can't understand his precipitous action. With his natural kindness and his passion to tell others about Jesus, he seemed well suited for the ministry. "What happened?" I ask.

"I'm no good at settling controversies or persuading people to do things," he replies. "I'm more of a follower than a leader."

"Mum would be so disappointed. She'd think it's God's will for you to stay at Ebenezer."

"It wouldn't make any difference," he retorts.

I can't help thinking that now even Jonathan has rebelled against her control of his spiritual life. Hoping to find a job in a lumber mill, he heads for Franklin, North Carolina, where Arlene's parents live.

While Jonathan and Dad start their new lives, Pierre Gousseland promotes me to senior vice president of AMAX. My new duties include investor relations, public relations, and publication of the annual report. The promotion brings a listing in *Who's Who in America* and a welcome increase in salary. But as I enjoy my higher standing in the company, I have almost forgotten the vision inspired by Martin Luther King.

One of the directors, Paul McAvoy, assistant dean of the Yale School of Management, tells me he wants to give some consulting fees to the university. "President Bart Giamatti used to be in my French class," I reply. "Why don't we invite him to lunch at Mory's? You can hand him the check."

At the next board meeting, Paul confides in wonder, "Bart doesn't want to eat at Mory's. He insists that we join him for lunch in the president's mansion and bring Pierre Gousseland."

I remember the last time I saw Bart at the lunch at Zeta Psi just before graduation. We talked then about our aspirations for the future. Almost twenty years later I still don't know where I'm going, although Giamatti, lucky guy, has already realized his presidential dream.

On the appointed day, Pierre and I drive to New Haven and pick up Paul MacAvoy in his office. We walk over to 43 Hillhouse Avenue, where Bart greets us warmly at the door. Remembering his scholarly interest in Milton's *Paradise Lost*, I say, "Congratulations on being restored to Paradise."

He chuckles. "This place is no Paradise."

The four of us sit down for lunch at an elegant table overlooking the garden. I launch into a discussion with Bart about the general apathy with regard to social issues when we were in college. I exclaim, "Back in the 1950s our classmates were more interested in drinking beer. Today students seem genuinely concerned."

Bart replies, "There were signs of growing interest, like the turnout for Martin Luther King Jr."

I catch my breath at his unexpected response. The photograph of me helping Martin Luther King Jr. cut his birthday cake lies buried in my filing cabinet at home. I recall my vow to help make the world a better place. Was it just youthful idealism? What have I done for other people?

As Pierre and I drive back to corporate headquarters, I remember my discussion at International House about young people who start out with great idealism and then give up because they can't change the world. At the time I said it would make more sense to follow the example of Dr. King with the Montgomery bus strike and try to change just that part of the world where we can make a difference. There's no opportunity in the office. Or is there?

A recent development comes to mind. A little known 1978 amendment to the Internal Revenue Code known as Section 401(k) enables workers to defer receiving a portion of their salary, which is instead contributed on their behalf, before taxes, to a savings plan. In other words, they can invest part of their paycheck in a thrift plan *using pretax* dollars. The legislation was effective January 1, 1980.

I think about my desire to help workers who change jobs but are unable to take their pensions with them. This unique program could be the answer. What's more, AMAX already has a defined contribution plan, known as the Thrift Plan, which could be used for that purpose.

Section 401(k) has never been utilized by a big industrial company like AMAX, but I suggest to Pierre, "If we amended the Thrift Plan to make it a 401(k) plan, employees would be able to use pretax dollars to save for their retirement. They would also continue to enjoy all the advantages of the Thrift Plan, including matching contributions, the ability to manage their own investments, and the right to take their benefits with them if they leave."

To my delight, Pierre says, "Send me a memorandum outlining your proposal." A few days later full of enthusiasm he reports, "I showed your memo to Bill Coleman and he likes the idea."

At a meeting of the compensation committee, Coleman, who is chairman, declares, "This will help our employees help themselves."

The board unanimously approves the amendment and the AMAX 401(k) becomes my responsibility. I quickly organize company-wide meetings to educate employees about the tax advantages of the new plan. I also initiate quarterly reports to participants about their pretax contributions and the performance of their investments. A secretary in the Denver office reflects the growing excitement about the plan. She says, "This could turn into something big!"

Thanks to the reminder by Bart Giamatti my dream of making a difference has come back to life. But instead of civil rights I focus on helping workers improve their financial security in retirement.

Pierre rewards my 401(k) initiative by making me a member of the Employee Benefit Portfolio Committee. The committee monitors the performance of investment managers running the company's pension fund. I remember my surprise at White & Case on discovering the Bankers Trust Company pension trust had a huge surplus, which enabled the bank to increase benefits. I find that AMAX has a similar surplus. Since the company bears the investment risk, any excess, after satisfying all liabilities, belongs to the company. An intriguing idea crosses my mind. Could we use the surplus to reduce corporate debt?

Pensions are not part of the traditional job of a corporate secretary, but my success with the 401(k) plan gives me credibility. I initiate long discussions with our outside counsel and our actuary. The actuary says, "This has never been attempted by a big corporation, but it could work."

Relishing my growing responsibilities, I linger in the office long after everyone one else has gone. My life becomes an endless round of lobbying, board meetings, and management crises. I return home exhausted. Most of the family stress Dad once absorbed falls on Carol. She says, "I want to support your career, but I wish you would help more with the children."

Carol goes to parent-teacher meetings, not me. She tells the guidance counselor that Debby has trouble completing her work. She persuades the school to give her extra time for assignments and tests. Even so, after dinner Debby insists, "You need to help me, before you read Jon's story or talk to Dad." Sometimes both Debby and Dave want help, and Carol spends two or three hours working on homework. I don't stop to think what a thankless task this must be for a stepmother.

Even Carol's warm relationship with Dave comes under pressure. Over six feet tall, he becomes increasingly argumentative. He has an annoying habit of leaving piles of dirty clothes on his bedroom floor. When Carol reproves him, he retorts, "They don't bother me."

"Well, they bother me," she replies. "So take them down to the laundry."

Muttering, he grabs an armful and thumps downstairs.

Dave causes havoc at school and at home, leaving us embarrassed and frustrated. One evening as I walk into the kitchen, I hear Carol yell, "Your bedroom smells of cigarette smoke."

"I left the window open," Dave replies defiantly.

She protests, "You know you have allergies. And it's against the rules."

"I don't care!" he shouts and stamps out.

Carol's face is white with indignation. She stares at me and insists, "He puts up an argument every time I ask him to do something. At age sixteen he needs to learn about rules and being considerate of others. Either he leaves or I will."

Later she turns angrily on me. "You don't appreciate what I do, and you don't give me any support. I can't take it anymore. I'm leaving."

She drives off in the car.

I can hardly breathe. Gulping for air, I relive the nightmare of Morganne leaving me. I remember the overwhelming pain, the guilt, the loneliness.

A few hours later she returns. I say humbly, "I'm sorry things are so difficult."

"If the children had not already lost their first mother, I would leave. But I don't want to do that to them," she replies. "I love them too much."

Her words shake me up. My job is taking me away from the children. Nine years ago when Carol took them on, she described them as "little lost souls," and she realizes their vulnerability more than I. With Dave so hard to manage and Carol so unhappy, I feel torn between family and career. Before I go to bed, I pray, "Lord, help me be a better husband and father." On Monday, though, as I drive into the executive parking area, I dream of getting yet more responsibility at work.

After further discussion with Carol, I tell Dave, "You have to go away to school for your own good and for all of us." We manage to enroll him at Gould Academy in Bethel, Maine, for the coming year under the watchful eye of a tough ex-marine house master.

Meanwhile, the business environment becomes ugly. Investment in capital goods dries up, and metals prices drop to new lows. There's not much management can do except cut back production and conserve cash. AMAX reports operating losses, and the board reduces and then eliminates the dividend. When Pierre orders a general reduction of corporate staff, he expects me to participate. I shudder. I've just moved up, and now I've got to fire five people whom I admire. It's awful.

However, my pension research pays off. I devise a radical plan to restructure the defined benefit plan and use the huge surplus to help AMAX through the downturn. It would free 100 million dollars to reduce corporate debt.

Pierre listens patiently to my proposal and authorizes me to take the restructuring to the board. He says, "I'll give you a minute or two to introduce the idea, but don't talk too long."

At the board meeting, a new director, Harold Brown, former secretary of defense under President Jimmy Carter, asks, "What will happen to the benefits for prior years?"

Pierre turns to me for the answer. I respond, "We're going to purchase the safest available annuities from a top-rated life insurance company."

President Ford asks, "How do the employees feel about the change?"

I reply confidently, "They like it, because there are benefit increases for everyone."

After a lengthy discussion, one of the Socal directors makes the motion. To my delight it carries unanimously. But a transaction of this kind has never received formal government approval. We have no guarantee we can make it happen.

# Chapter Nineteen

## *A PENSION BATTLE IN WASHINGTON INSPIRES A NEW DREAM*

At first I don't know where to go for approval of the pension restructuring. I approach the Treasury, the Department of Labor, and the Pension Benefit Guarantee Corporation known as the PBGC. I discover the PBGC has jurisdiction. With the blessing of Pierre Gousseland, I fly down to Washington in the corporate jet to join Bill Coleman for urgent meetings with the agency.

In the midst of my campaign, I discover Senator Howard Metzenbaum—a Democrat closely allied with the labor movement— opposes pension reversions. He wants to change the law so the excess will go to the participants in the plan, not the company. He proposes a moratorium on reversions. To broaden the offensive, I arrange for Bill Coleman to speak at a meeting of the Labor Policy Association in Williamsburg. He says, "It's a voluntary system. If companies can't take money out of pension plans, they won't put it in." The members of the Labor Policy Association agree. I urge them to lobby their friends in the White House and the Senate.

While I lobby for the pension restructuring I also monitor the AMAX 401(k) plan. My staff reports that employees delight in the pretax contributions, the company match, and the growth of their portfolio. They know the money belongs to them and if they change jobs, they can take it with them. It will improve their financial security in retirement.

I encourage my allies in the Labor Policy Association to offer 401(k) plans. But I discover to my dismay that some employers resist adopting plans out of fear of liability for the investment decisions of their employees. I wonder what would Martin Luther King Jr. do?

The battle in Washington impacts my life at home, but I don't worry about that. As an officer of a Fortune 200 company, how can I expect anything else? While I try to grab a few hours' sleep before the July board meeting, the phone rings. It's Christopher. "Dave and I are at the Port Chester police station. Please pick us up."

Half-awake, without a second thought, I say, "Just a minute, here's your mother."

Carol gets dressed. She doesn't complain. She knows I expect her to take care of the children because of the pressures of my job. The boys tell us they had sneaked out of the house after we went to bed and gotten a ride to a Tex-Mex restaurant in the neighboring town of Port Chester. A policeman, who noticed an unopened case of beer in their car, took them back to the station and said, "Call your parents."

On hearing about Carol driving to the police station in a dangerous area late at night, her mother protests indignantly, "Their father should have picked them up."

I ignore the criticism and reassure Carol. "Life will settle down once Dave returns to Gould Academy." But soon after Dave's departure, Carol announces, "I want to have another baby."

"Why?" I ask in dismay.

She explains, "I've always wanted two children of my own. I told you that when we were courting."

Her insistence takes me by surprise. I protest, "But we already have our hands full."

She sits on the edge of the bed and looks up at me. "I loved being pregnant and nursing my own baby."

Still unconvinced, I demand, "What about the cost?"

She pleads, "That's not the point. I wouldn't have married you if you had told me I couldn't have two children. If I have to go back to work to help pay for college, I will."

The following day I shut the door to my office and ask my secretary to hold any calls. In the uneasy, fateful silence, I pray, "Lord, you know how I feel. Help me make the right decision." I remember what Carol has done for the older children, and I want to make her happy. Given my successful career, surely I can handle the bills. I resolve to have another child for her sake.

One glorious fall weekend we decide to drive down to Virginia to visit the Masins. Chris pleads for permission to remain behind with a friend. After our return I find a lot of beer cans behind the garage. One of our neighbors says ominously, "The guests at our dinner party were amused by all the excitement at your house last Saturday."

Carol asks, "What are you talking about?"

"All those police cruisers going in and out of your driveway," he replies.

We confront Christopher, who claims a rumor of a party spread through the high school like wildfire. Before long over two hundred teenagers poured in, looking for a good time. He became worried about damage and set off the burglar alarm. After the police arrived, many youngsters left, but the players from the high school football team camped out on the back lawn with their girlfriends. Some of them objected to the charge for beer imposed by a student entrepreneur. When they started to rip the quarter panels off the poor fellow's car, Chris panicked and called the station house. Two more squad cars screamed up with lights flashing.

How embarrassing! What do the neighbors think?

Carol and I conclude Chris agrees with our rules, but then does what he wants behind our backs. Although he has always been a strong student, he now seems sidetracked by his social life. I tell him, "A good boarding school will help you realize your full potential."

While we search for the right school, Senator Metzenbaum renews his call for a moratorium on pension reversions. I receive a summons to a meeting with the PBGC in Washington. Bill Coleman joins me while I explain that the company intends to increase benefits for all participants under the plan before we take out the excess funds. The director makes no commitment but promises to send the issue to the Cabinet Council.

As Bill Coleman and I head over to the White House to talk with the chairman of the Council of Economic Advisers about pension reversions I also give him an update on the AMAX 401(k) plan. I can't help speculating whether I could apply the lessons I have learned in this lobbying campaign to expand the 401(k) program.

Between trips to Washington, I take a day off to drive Chris for an interview at Mount Hermon School in Massachusetts, which was founded by the same Dwight Moody who started Moody Bible Institute. Wonderfully at home, I walk through dormitories built with funds from revival meetings in England in the 1870s. All the students have jobs. I tell Chris, "I remember playing rugby here for Yale against Dartmouth." To my delight, he agrees to enroll.

Chris plays lacrosse for Mount Hermon, makes honors, and becomes a student leader. He finds courage to express his feeling about his mother's death in an essay, "To Steal a Child's Heart," which he sends me.

> My brother and I arose to the soft footsteps gliding down the stairs. Curious, we both pounced out of bed. In my bare feet and my baby-blue pajamas, I trotted down the hall to my parents' room and peered in through the cracked open door. Noticing the ever-warm presence of my mother missing, I started down the long wooden steps with my brother at my heels. As we walked into the kitchen, I watched the old brown station wagon I knew so well lumber out the driveway. Puzzled, I walked over to the low kitchen window and peered out into the colorful new day. My brother and I gazed out the window for an eternity while part of my heart flew peacefully to the clouds. As the moment was marked in my mind with a tear, I noticed a midsummer's leaf fall to the ground.

Memories of that terrible day flood back. I sit and weep as I feel his pain.

I want my family to be happy. Family happiness for me was symbolized by my holidays at Kington Mead Farm. I love the land the way so many of my kin, past and present, do. Farms have always made me happy. I begin to think, why not use my successful career to obtain the Virginia equivalent of Kington Mead?

A few days before Carol's due date, Pierre schedules a strategy session at a conference center in Armonk, New York. Carol protests, "I'm afraid you won't leave the meeting if I go into labor." As I listen to a forecast for the price of molybdenum, I imagine her holding an alarm clock and struggling to control her breathing without me to coach her. I bury my head in my hands in shame.

Sure enough, in the middle of the conference, Carol sends a message. "The baby's coming. I'm going to the hospital."

I rush out of the meeting. When I reach her bedside, I find her panting in labor. She gasps, "Thank goodness, you're here!"

I sit close and look at the minute hand on my watch repeating at intervals. "You're getting near the peak. You're at the peak! You're past the peak." Sweat builds up on her forehead as she concentrates on her breathing. We don't know until after the baby's delivered that the umbilical cord was looped twice around his neck, threatening strangulation.

I shudder to think we almost lost our baby. We call him Thomas after Dad's father, who owned Sunny Bank in England.

Carol delights in breast-feeding Thomas. She finds a capable young lady named Claire to help with the children and the housework. As life settles down, I remind her of the toast we made with the Masins to a farm in Virginia. She asks, "How are you going to pay for it?"

I reply, "It would be possible if we sold Sunny Bank, which has appreciated considerably in value, and move to a smaller house in Greenwich. We would have no trouble in obtaining a mortgage."

She hesitates, "We already have too much debt. Besides, I want to enjoy my baby."

I plead, and reluctantly she agrees to let me search.

I find Windsor Farm with 218 acres of beautiful rolling land at the foot of the Blue Ridge Mountains. The manor house dating from 1789 has seven fireplaces. An old smokehouse guards a boxwood garden and a pool of goldfish. In the fall the Piedmont Hunt meets in home field.

With our four-month-old Thomas in a carry basket, I take Carol to see it. We drive on a dirt road past Black Angus cattle grazing peacefully in open fields with sturdy black fences. Clouds scud across the blue December sky. Oak and maple trees line the circular driveway, and a white frost covers the front lawn. Carol carefully lifts Thomas, who is sound asleep, puts him under a blanket in the carry basket, and sets it down on a bench. I was about the same age when my parents took me to Kington Mead Farm for the first time.

Windsor Farm is exactly what I have been looking for. It could become a family homestead and give all of us great joy. I know Carol's pleasure with her baby has a lot to do with her willingness to consider buying a farm in Virginia. With a burst of emotion, I declare, "This is close to my heart, just as having Thomas is close to yours."

After thinking about it, she looks steadily at me and says, "If this will make you happy, go for it!"

She finds a smaller house in a residential area of Greenwich on Long Island Sound called Belle Haven. It's only five minutes from the office. She likes the area because the homes are close together, providing us a greater sense of community than in the back country. There are more families with children nearby. We already belong to the Belle Haven Club. Determinedly, I negotiate a complex game of Monopoly, buying and selling houses in Greenwich simultaneously with buying a farm in Virginia.

My perseverance in the pension battle is rewarded by the White House. President Reagan's Cabinet Council approves pension restructuring. I testify at a hearing of the Senate Labor subcommittee where the new policy is announced. Since I fought for the policy, it seems like a badge of honor to be questioned extensively by Senator Metzenbaum. We apply 100 million dollars from the pension surplus to reduce corporate debt. I assume in due time my contribution will be recognized with a promotion and an increase in salary.

As I reflect on our triumph, a new dream begins to crystallize in my mind. Why not enlist Bill Coleman and the Labor Policy Association to lobby the administration to eliminate the road block to the expansion of 401(k) plans? This is something I can do for America.

# Chapter Twenty

## *MUM'S SECRET*

When the time comes for listing AMAX on the London Stock Exchange, I want to arrange a celebration in London for UK shareholders. I remember that Jane, the daughter of Mum's sister Auntie Joyce, married a solicitor named Gordon Jones. I ask Gordon to help organize a lunch for the investment community and the press at venerable Goldsmiths' Hall.

After the shareholder meeting, Jane and Gordon invite me to dinner at their home in Putney with another of our cousins, Auntie Joan's daughter Ruth. Jane conducts us briskly to the dining room and instructs us where to sit. Her confident face and take-charge manner remind me of Mum. And I forget about Martin Luther King Jr. and 401(k) plans. As Gordon offers a glass of claret, we discuss the family past.

I am not surprised to hear that in our mothers' childhoods, Granny Hadley often went off to London leaving her children to fend for themselves. Mum, who was the eldest, had to prepare the meals. But the real shock comes when Cousin Ruth describes what happened when Granny was at home.

At the time her mother was seven and Mum was fourteen, a family friend from the Gloucester Rowing Club would arrive at The Lawn in his gleaming new Humber to take Granny Hadley for a ride. Granny insisted on taking Joan with them and instructed her to bring her favorite book. On arrival at "Uncle Bert's" bungalow on the Gloucester-

Sharpness canal, Granny told Joan to stay in the car and read. Granny and Uncle Bert went inside. Sometimes Joan got out of the car, but she knew she mustn't go near the bungalow.

Unsettled by this story, I wonder if Joan went home and complained to her big sister about the boring long wait. Did she ask, "What were they doing in there?" How naïve would Mum have been at fourteen? Wouldn't suspicion have bitten?

Why did Mum go on to act so differently from her sisters? Why did she become a missionary instead of marrying an eligible young man like they did? What turned her away from the course of her affluent upbringing? Such questions never occurred to me as a boy, but now I'm stumbling across part of Mum's life that she kept hidden.

When I return home and pack for the move to our new house in Belle Haven, I discover Dad has left Mum's childhood photo album. I find a picture of a tall man standing in front of the bungalow on the canal. The caption underneath the photograph in Mum's neat handwriting says, "Uncle Bert."

I remember my Australian cousin Geoffrey mentioned someone with the same name. Suddenly, I am determined to know more. I call Dad and ask, "Who was Uncle Bert?"

"He was Granny Hadley's friend."

"Was he more than a friend?"

Dad pauses for what seems like a long time. "I suppose it won't hurt to tell you now. There was an incident at The Lawn when your mother was at grammar school. She came home early and found Granny and Bert in the summerhouse by the tennis court."

He adds in a sober voice, "She was shocked out of her mind!"

"How awful," I exclaim. "That explains a lot."

After a moment of ominous silence, Dad continues, "Your grandfather was just as bad. At the end of his life, he had a lady on Calton Road. He was riding his bike home from visiting her when he had his heart attack."

Dad's revelation shakes me. How painful the knowledge of her parents' mutual betrayal must have been to Mum. Now I know why she never talked about life as a teenager. I wince as I imagine a bewildered young girl trying to cope with what she witnessed in the summerhouse. The shameful secret must have preyed on her like the mosquitoes did later in the Indian rainforest. Whom could she talk to? How did she keep going?

I realize that it must have been soon after this time that she became friends with the kindhearted Woodruff family who went to Brunswick Road Baptist church. At one of the services she attended with them, she experienced conversion. Soon after she was baptized and became a fervent member of the church. The assurance of her new faith must have helped her survive her trauma, although the scar clearly lasted for life.

It seems she never lost a subconscious rage at her parents. The clues were there, but I had never put it all together before. She gave only curt answers to my questions about Grandpa's achievements in sports and business, although I believe she was proud of them. She withheld affection from Granny until the end.

I believe I saw traces of the trauma in the sharp edge of her zeal when she lashed out at me with guilt-creating accusations. She didn't want me to go in the same direction as her father and mother, so she dedicated me to the Lord. With all the force of her dominating personality, she focused on making her firstborn a recompense for her terrible secret. Even after I became a lawyer and a businessman, she never stopped trying to impose her will. I recognize sadly the sins of her parents were visited on us both.

But I have never thought about life from her point of view before. What was it like for her as a young mother trying to keep her babies safe while German bombers flew over Gloucester? How easy was it for her at age sixty-four to give up the church in Attica, where she was happy, to rescue me and care for my three devastated children after Morganne died? Didn't she share my pain? The more I think about it, the more I realize her love for me was deep and abiding.

After I finish packing, I sit in my black leather chair in the library with Mum's photo album. Now that I understand what triggered those guilt-laden accusations, it's time to leave the sting and bitterness behind. I don't want any anger left between us. I whisper, "Mum, I forgive you," and at last I begin to cry, sobbing hard in my hands. I'm crying for Mum and for myself.

# Chapter Twenty-One

## *THE KICK*

I need a trustworthy manager for Windsor Farm. He will look after the tenants, keep the fences in repair, and bush-hog the fields. With a flash of inspiration, I think of my brother, Jonathan, who is unhappy in his lumberyard job in North Carolina. Arlene would like to live nearer to their children in Michigan and Pennsylvania. Carol and I fly to Franklin to discuss the possibility of their joining our venture and helping on the farm.

Now that I feel positive about Mum, I remember her enthusiasm for family gatherings. I know she would encourage me to share Windsor Farm with Jonathan. However, her memory prompts me to emphasize, "If you ever want to return to the ministry, it would be okay with me."

"It's not likely," he replies.

We successfully close our real-estate transactions and move to our new home in Belle Haven. The weather roasts hot and humid, but inside the house seems cool, with a pleasant breeze off the water. From the kitchen window we look out at boats rocking at anchor in the harbor. After taking seven-year-old Jon sailing for the first time, Carol says enthusiastically, "It reminds me of sailing in Hong Kong with my father."

Despite the carefree, almost holiday, atmosphere at home, a wisp of uncertainty drifts across the AMAX horizon. The board, impatient with the share price and the financial condition of the company, brings in a new president named Al Born. The heir apparent negotiates for a huge compensation package, and Pierre asks me to check the numbers provided by Born with regard to his previous compensation. I give a favorable report.

Earlier in his career he worked for an AMAX mining subsidiary out west. I hear rumors he had a difficult relationship with some of the senior officers of the company, but since I don't know him, I pay no attention. He seems like a worthy candidate because of his operating experience.

I try to develop a relationship with him while remaining loyal to my friend Pierre, who is still chief executive. Al keeps pushing to take over total responsibility. At one point he says to me, "You're the only person I talk to about this."

While Al Born strains to take charge of AMAX, my brother, Jonathan, arrives with Arlene to assume his responsibilities at Windsor Farm. He asks, "Dave, how am I going to learn about farming?" Good question!

Since his predecessor works nearby, I suggest hopefully, "Why don't you offer to help Chubby, the old manager? He'll tell you everything." The strategy works. Grateful to have an extra man digging holes for a line of fence posts, Chubby coaches Jonathan in his new position.

Dad comes over from England with Sylvia to see my new manager in action. We all go for a long hike across the stream and through the fields. Dad says, "I'm amazed my son could own such a place."

We stop at the equipment shed to watch my brother operate the front-end loader on a tractor. Arlene confides, "Jonathan is so happy. All the stress from the lumberyard has gone. He's like a new man."

When Al Born finally takes over as chief executive, I alert him to another opportunity to reduce corporate debt by using excess pension funds in various subsidiaries of the company. He authorizes me to proceed. I restructure these plans, one subsidiary at a time. We raise another 100 million dollars.

As corporate secretary I help Al with detailed agendas and carefully crafted talking points for board meetings. I also initiate an interview with The New York Times and organize a press conference in London for him, which result in favorable coverage. But I don't know where I stand on his team. I decide to bide my time on the campaign to change the rules governing 401(k) plans until I feel more secure.

He suggests I move from the secretary's department at the back corner of the top floor of corporate headquarters to a front office near his. Foolishly, I hesitate because I don't want to be separated from my staff. Later I realize I've made a huge mistake.

The day after the June 1986 board meeting, Al walks into my office. He's never done this before. He asks why the compensation committee didn't give him a salary increase after six months as chairman. He's angry. Perhaps he thinks I should have put more pressure on Bill Coleman.

His question raises a red flag, and I realize I need to concentrate on my job. Despite my acknowledged valuable contribution to the survival of the company, he offers no recognition and I receive no promotion. I try to repress my bitter disappointment.

I escape to Windsor Farm for a family reunion attended by Dad and Sylvia. Crowding into the dining room in the basement, we pepper our meals with speeches and jokes. We splash through hot afternoons in the pool and compete in Family Olympics organized by my nephew, Jeffrey.

Twenty-one of us gather on the back porch for a Sunday morning service conducted by Dad with Sylvia dutifully playing a portable organ borrowed for the occasion. He invites my brother, Jonathan, to pray and asks Ruth to read from the Bible. He preaches to his assembled family about one of his favorite texts, "Ebenezer ... Hitherto hath the Lord helped us."

Dad explains that Samuel put up a memorial stone called Ebenezer, to remind the children of Israel of God's help in the past and to encourage them to trust God in the future. He says, "A lot has happened in the years since we arrived in America. As you look back, think of your education, your jobs, your partners, and your families. In our joys and in our sorrows we can all say Ebenezer." I know he's right. I should rejoice that Windsor Farm has become a safe and secure place where our friendship can flourish.

Back home Debby says, "Perhaps the Lord wanted you to do this for the family. Although you thought you were buying the farm for yourself, you were really buying it to unite us."

When I return to work on Monday morning, I go see Al Born about some corporate housekeeping matters. As I turn to leave, he gives me a cold-blooded look and says in a hard voice, "Now I'm going to bust your ass."

In a split second he dynamites my much-loved job. By "busting my ass" he means to take away my responsibilities as corporate secretary and bury me alive in a new group called Central Services. It's the back office. His brutal words convey a pent-up anger I don't understand, a cruelty that has no feeling for the service I have given.

A sharp pain shoots through my stomach. I know in that moment my career is doomed. I helped the company survive a financial crisis, and I ought to be promoted, not demoted. With my knees shaking, I ask him in a faint voice, "Why are you doing this?"

He replies coldly, in language that sounds as if it has been rehearsed with a lawyer, "This is the new form of management that I want to put into place."

After putting it off for several days, I finally tell Carol the bad news. She says loyally, "It's unfair. Go back and ask him again what you've done to deserve such treatment."

With my head down, I return to his office to appeal to his sense of fairness. He offers me special benefits if I retire. I think bitterly, how could I retire at age fifty-one with five children heading for college? My head reels at the injustice. I can't believe he would do this to me.

Carol shivers when she hears his response. "What if something happens to you? How will we survive? We've got these enormous mortgages on two places ..."

I feel the same alarm about the mortgages, but I don't want to admit it was a mistake to buy the farm.

Carol must have had second thoughts because later she leaves a note by the bed. "I do love you and appreciate all you have done for me. You're a wonderful husband and father and a good provider. Please take care of yourself and your health. We all love you so much."

In desperation I call several headhunters. No one is interested.

As I stagger from the shock, I realize Al Born might be jealous of my long and close relationship with the directors. Perhaps he moved me to the back office because he was afraid to fire me. But I must make the best of it. I don't dare seek the help of my friends on the board.

Deeply wounded, I take the minutes at the next board meeting in the Pan Am building in New York. Al Born brings up the election of a member of my staff, who is an assistant secretary, to take my place. To my surprise, the chairman of the finance committee objects to her lack of experience. I should know at this point it would be wise for me to remain silent, but I can't help myself. Out of instinct ingrained from years of helping the chairman pursue his agenda, I volunteer, "She's fully qualified."

It's my last board meeting.

As I ride the elevator down, a sympathetic director asks, "How do you feel about the change in your responsibilities?" I rub my eyes and stare at the floor. I don't want to criticize Al Born because I need my job.

I don't need to explain the calamity to Bill Coleman. He says about Al Born, "He's taken away all your power." Coming from Bill, who I counted on to help me extend 401(k) plans to workers with no pensions, this hurts. I realize, to my dismay, I have lost the chance to lead a lobbying campaign.

Now even the best of times are laced with foreboding. Carol organizes a fiftieth birthday party at the farm inviting our local friends. She proposes a toast, which I find moving, because she seldom expresses her feelings openly. I want to celebrate, but I sit there in repressed silence. With fear gnawing in my bowels, I can't even talk with a friend from Trinity Church sitting next to me.

I know I must try to make the best of my new position as president of AMAX Central Services. The recovery of excess funds from the pension plans of AMAX subsidiaries nears an end. But one opportunity remains. A fifty-percent-owned affiliate called Alumax needs money for a critical capital expenditure. I nervously point out to Al Born that Alumax has an overfunded plan. He obtains the approval of the other shareholder and authorizes me to submit a proposal to the AMAX board. This is my last pension reversion.

By the end of 1987, the total recovery amounts to $245 million. This huge infusion of cash helps AMAX survive one of the worst crises in its history. It not only benefits the shareholders, it also benefits Al Born. In 1988 metals prices start to recover, and after a three-year hiatus the board restores the dividend. I keep hoping for some recognition, but it never comes. Instead, Born instructs me to report to Tom McKeever, the new president and second in charge.

My new supervisor says, "You're lucky to have a job. Five other senior officers have been terminated." After six months he hands me a performance appraisal as president of AMAX Central Services. He verifies that I've cleaned up the mess in the back office and grades my performance as "outstanding." But he adds, "There's nowhere for you to go. You're vulnerable."

I reply nervously, "I'd love to be head of an operating division."

He looks me in the eye. "You'd be less exposed if you took a pay cut and resigned as a corporate officer."

"Why is there a need to emasculate me any further?" I ask. "I've been an officer for fourteen years. I'm doing a good job." Although I desperately struggle to hang on, I know I'm being forced out.

Life becomes stressful at home as Dave gets in scrapes and struggles in and out of college. Eventually, he settles down at Castleton State College in Vermont, not far from Stratton, where we used to ski.

Tension builds in Debby's last year at Greenwich High School. She still wants help with homework every night. After slogging through English, French, history, and math, one evening Carol sighs, "Despite all my efforts, she never seems to appreciate what I do for her."

To our astonishment, Debby tells the guidance counselor at school no one ever helps with her homework. This annoys Carol so much she refuses to continue. Debby spends a lot of time secluded in her room, talking on the telephone with friends. Their parents tell us she complains about the way she is treated by her stepmother.

Carol urges me to spend more time with my daughter so I take her on trips to see the paintings at the Frick Collection and the Metropolitan Museum. Every day I drive her to school. Once a week we stop for breakfast at Le Peep restaurant on Greenwich Avenue. She wants to talk about her birth mother. I gradually realize her loss was different from her brothers. She was abandoned by a mother she can't remember. I need to share with her more completely my memories of Morganne.

In August 1987 Debby enters Denison University in Granville, Ohio. To my delight, on parents' weekend she invites me to watch her play rugby for Denison.

Christopher also plays rugby. I shudder when he is knocked out playing for Vassar against Army. He is elected to Phi Beta Kappa. He remembers my reason for sending him to Mount Hermon and says, "Dad, do you think I've reached my full potential?"

Now that all three of Morganne's children have left home, Dad writes optimistically, "After your many 'trials,' may they bring you much happiness and blessing." However, much as I love my children, I have become wary about hoping for anything.

Carol has her own perspective. She enrolls in graduate school at Manhattanville College and writes a paper about the difficulty created by the stereotype of the "wicked stepmother." She argues that the most a stepmother can realistically hope for is a relationship of mutual liking and respect. However, she concludes, "In many instances love does grow."

Thank goodness for my brother, Jonathan. Breathing the sweet smell of freshly cut hay, we investigate an offer by a neighbor to purchase some of the lumber in our woods. As we walk past my neighbor's Black Angus cattle grazing near the stream, he says, "Dave, when you're not around, I feel as if I own the place."

"That's fine with me," I reply. "I'm so lucky to have you here."

Even chatting with him on the phone about painting a tenant house or buying a new manure spreader gives me vicarious pleasure. We muddle through the problems with the same trust in each other that we had riding our bikes to school in Gloucester in the fog. When I ask him to exercise our two horses, he responds gamely, "I'll give it a try."

One day he invites Jon to join him for a ride to Piney Swamp. Leading the way on Kington, he keeps turning to joke with his nephew. They cross the stream and trot gently up the slope. Suddenly, Kington jumps like a bronco. My brother hangs on desperately, but when Kington rears he shoots into the air. He seems to float for a moment, arms stretched to each side like a stuntman doing a swan dive. At the last moment, he whips his hands in front to save himself and skids forward on the wet ground just short of a fence post.

Jon calls out, "Are you all right, Uncle Jonathan? Kington got stung on the butt."

In the morning I see my brother riding Kington into the back field with Somerly on a lead rope. The dear old boy keeps his eyes straight ahead and his hands firmly on the reins. I don't tell him about the disaster at work.

In July 1988, Carol and I take the family to the Spartan program run by Skull and Bones on Deer Island in the St. Lawrence River. Since the island has no telephone or television set, we must create our own entertainment. We begin each day with a quick swim in the cold river led by Paul Lambert, a gregarious New York lawyer, who was volunteering in George H. W. Bush's campaign for the presidency. While we watch the fireworks over Boldt Castle on Independence Day, Paul says, "Why don't you get involved in the campaign in Connecticut?"

The suggestion prompts me to listen to George Bush speaking on television at the Republican Convention. He talks about a kinder and gentler nation. He sounds like a good man. Carol and I decide to attend a campaign fundraiser in the home of a friend from St. Barnabas. We briefly meet George and Barbara Bush in the crush. In September we attend the opening of the Bush-Quayle headquarters in Stamford where we chat with the vice president's brother, Prescott Bush, and his wife Beth.

Since I'm not so busy at work these days, I offer to write a talk for Prescott to give at a forum at Christchurch in Greenwich in October. I study his brother's acceptance speech at the Republican Convention about "economic empowerment" and "opportunity." He said, "Power must always be kept close to the individual, close to the hands that raised the family and run the home… There is a God and he is good, and his love, while free, has a self-imposed cost: We must be good to one another."

This seems to tie in with a verse I studied at Moody: 1 Timothy 5:8. "If any provide not for his own, and specially for those of his own house, he hath denied the faith." I draft a talk quoting this text. "We must accept our responsibilities to ourselves, to our families, and to our neighbors. We cannot pass them off to society or the government. Freedom without responsibility is no freedom at all."

Pres says, "It's a crackerjack speech."

Strangely enough, what I most enjoyed about the research was finding the Bible back in the center of my life. How ironic when, crippled with humiliation and fear for the future, I'm again feeling

I have done little to help other people. Have I forgotten the dream inspired by Martin Luther King Jr.?

I head for the phone bank after work and make thousands of phone calls to voters in southwestern Connecticut. To my delight, other members of the family join the campaign. For an article in a conservative Vassar student magazine, *The Right Angle,* which he helped establish, Chris interviews Prescott Bush. Carol places an ad about the vice president in *Greenwich Time* with the slogan, "If you're going to change horses in midstream, don't switch to one going in the other direction."

*David and Carol with Vice President George H. W. Bush and Barbara Bush in Greenwich in 1988 during the campaign.*

We drive with Beth Bush to a rally at Fairfield University. Jon makes a sign that says, BUSH OR BUST. We sit high in the bleachers with thousands of cheering supporters and marvel at five bands playing at the same time. Thomas, who is four, looks down at the action and says, "Dad, is this a circus?"

However, enjoyment of the campaign is overshadowed by cutthroat politics at AMAX. On Monday, October 24, 1988, Al Born's promise to "bust my ass" is carried out.

Tom McKeever summons me and offers a cup of coffee. I decline. He says, "The company has decided to terminate you. You must leave the building now and stay away. Until June, we'll give you a temporary office at another location."

My career at AMAX is over. I remember with compassion those employees I fired in 1981.

# Chapter Twenty-Two

## THE LABOR SECRETARY'S QUESTION

George H. W. Bush wins the election, carrying Connecticut by 74,000 votes or six percent of the total. We're delighted, but I'm sick with anxiety about my own future.

Dad and Sylvia arrive on their annual visit. With a dull pain throbbing in my head, I confide, "I've been fired. I'm looking for another job."

Dad replies reassuringly, "When one door closes, the Lord will open another door."

AMAX gives me a farewell lunch at the Belle Haven Club. Al Born sits on my right, in front of the crowd that used to report to me. Although he has fired me, I want him there to reduce my embarrassment. I'm determined to remain in control, but three lines into my speech, my lip trembles and I flounder in a way I barely understand. During the war I learned to repress fear, but now I choke up and pause frequently for breath. I try to mean it when I say, "I believe this is a country of opportunity ... and the promise ... which was there for me years ago ... is still there today ... for all of us." After lunch I hurry away. Devastated by the train wreck of my career, I want to conceal how much I hurt.

My sister, Ruth, offers comfort. She writes, "You and the company have benefited each other and can part in mutual gratitude ... In the end, the only reckoning that matters is the one we each make in our deepest selves." But although I know I gave the best of my working self, I don't have peace.

I fear that everybody in Greenwich will hear I've been terminated. And what about the bills? How am I going to pay the bills? As I retreat past my temporary secretary to my temporary office, I try not to show I'm afraid.

A friend of mine at St. Barnabas resigns his job as an investment banker at Morgan Stanley to train for the ministry. I wonder if I too should apply to divinity school.

Since we moved to Belle Haven, we have attended a church in the center of the town instead of making the long drive to St. Barnabas. As a result, we don't seem to belong anywhere. Utterly miserable, I struggle through each day, just as I did when Morganne died. Back then I found comfort in prayer and the story of Job. But unlike Job I have pursued my ambition at the expense of my ideals.

Saturday morning in mid-December looms dark with a thunderstorm. Humiliated and dismayed by my own shortcomings and the unfairness of my termination, I remember how Martin Luther King Jr. responded to terrifying threats to his life. In *Stride toward Freedom* he described how, exhausted and depressed, he took his problem to God. I feel just as desperate.

I get on my knees beside my bed and put my face in my hands. The very act of breathing in and breathing out makes me more aware of God's presence. I speed through a long tunnel, going back in time. Sitting third row from the front at Trinity Baptist Church in Gloucester, I used to cover my face in the same way to shut out the world while I talked to God. Now my breath feels warm on my cheeks and eyes, just as it did when I was a child. In my wretchedness I sob, "Lord, I've been such an idiot. Please forgive me. Help me to find the way out of this blackness."

Thunder cracks and rain beats against the window. In the shelter of my praying hands, I feel relief from my pain.

A month later on January 20, 1989, George Bush takes the oath of office as the forty-first president. His relationship with Congress looks extraordinarily difficult because the Democrats control both the House of Representatives and the Senate. I note that he nominates Elizabeth Dole, wife of Senate Minority Leader Bob Dole, as secretary of labor.

As I mail out my résumé to the business community, I notice in the newspaper a "silent committee" advises the president-elect on political appointees. It includes the pollster Bob Teeter, the new Chief of Staff John Sununu, and the president's son George. I don't know George W. Bush, but he's a member of Skull and Bones. I wonder if I should try to get in touch with him about service in the new administration.

The chances of a political appointment are slim, and who in their right mind would ever want such a job? You take a lot of punishment and receive relatively little compensation for your pain. I would make twice as much in the private sector. On the other hand, money never deterred me from considering the ministry. Why should it deter me from public service? I need to discern if that is what God wants me to do with my life.

I ring the transition office and leave a message for George W. Bush. To my astonishment, he returns my phone call. I don't know what to say, so I mention I've just been elected a director of our society.

He focuses on an issue that has divided the directors and the membership for years and asks, "What do you think about the admission of women?"

I didn't expect to get into this. With some trepidation, I reply, "I believe the admission of women will strengthen the program."

Silence! I have no idea what George W. Bush thinks. He doesn't say. He simply moves on. "Why did you call?"

"To let you know I worked in your father's campaign and I'm interested in public service."

"What do you want?"

"I'd like to be secretary of the cabinet. I've had years of experience as a corporate secretary."

"It's gone. What else?"

I can't think of anything else and I don't know what to talk about. After a brief awkward moment, he hangs up. I could kick myself. I've blown my chance for a position in the Bush administration.

In a last desperate attempt to explore my options, I call Prescott Bush. His wife, Beth, answers the phone so I tell her about my interest in public service. She replies, "Pres is in China, but when we talk, I'll ask him to fax John Sununu."

Pres sends the fax as Beth promised, and Sununu sends back a noncommittal response. However, a few days later the mailman delivers a form letter from the transition office, asking about my involvement in the campaign and my interest in government service. I've learned from my conversation with George W. Bush I need to be specific, so I turn for help to my friend Paul Lambert. He lends me *The Prune Book: The 100 Toughest Management and Policy-Making Jobs in Washington* by John Trattner. A glance reveals one job where I have a lot of experience. It carries the title assistant secretary of labor for pension and welfare benefits. I would have jurisdiction over 401(k) plans. I list the position on the questionnaire.

One fateful afternoon as I frantically pour out more résumés, I receive a phone call from someone named Rod DeArment. He says, "Mrs. Dole has asked me to interview various people and your name is on the list. Are you interested in the position of assistant secretary of labor for pension and welfare benefits?"

I say emphatically, "Yes!"

He tells me to come down to Washington for an interview.

On February 14, Valentine's Day, I arrive early for my 10:00 AM appointment full of nervous excitement. Rod, who once served as chief of staff for Senate Minority Leader Bob Dole, is now Elizabeth Dole's choice for deputy secretary of labor. He tells me to come back at five o'clock. I spend the day cooling my heels in the National Gallery across the street.

At five o'clock an assistant immediately ushers me in to see Mrs. Dole. She stands to greet me with a welcoming smile. "Before you sit down, let me show you something. My predecessors always placed their desks with their back to the window. I moved my desk to this side of the room to face the other way." She points through the window to the floodlit Capitol. "As long as the lights are on in the Capitol, I know I don't need to rush home to make dinner for my husband."

I stare at the awesome view. I can't believe this is happening.

Once we sit down, she asks, "Why are you interested in public service?"

"My father is a minister and my mother was a missionary," I reply. "I started out following in my father's footsteps, but I became a lawyer."

Her face lights up as if she has recognized an old friend. She says, "I'm so glad you told me your mother was a missionary because I have a sense of mission about public service."

I sit bolt upright. I didn't expect to be talking about Mum in an interview. Elizabeth Dole makes it feel natural.

She looks at me intently. "What is your mission, David?" She seems to be asking me about my spiritual life. Is it still in second place to my career?

I reply, "My parents taught me it was a good thing to help other people."

She accepts my answer. Before I have a chance to elaborate about Martin Luther King Jr. and 401(k) plans, her assistant comes in to signal the end of the interview. As I leave I exclaim, "I'd really like to work for you."

Her assistant must have noticed her smile because he says, "You two seem to have hit it off!"

As I ride the train back to Greenwich, I shake my head in disbelief. After a lifetime of warfare, Mum has come to the rescue. I can hear her saying, "Praise the Lord!" She failed to march me into the ministry, and yet ironically, she had a positive impact on Elizabeth Dole.

But will I get the job? Anxiously, I contact Bill Coleman for advice. At his suggestion, I talk with President Ford, who promises to write to Mrs. Dole. I also seek out Ian MacGregor, my old boss at AMAX, when he speaks at the chamber of commerce in Greenwich. He too agrees to send a supporting letter.

Two weeks later, in the middle of another wave of résumés, Mrs. Dole calls. She says, "I'm pleased to offer you the position of assistant secretary of labor, subject, of course, to confirmation by the Senate."

I strain forward at my desk. "When would you like me to start?"

"As soon as possible! My assistant will be in touch with you about the paperwork."

I gleefully toss my résumés on the floor and rush home. Carol smiles as if she always expected something to work out. She throws her arms around my neck and gives me an affectionate kiss.

Since Mrs. Dole asked me to keep it confidential for a few days, we don't tell anybody. But I know a subcabinet position like this carries a lot of clout. I wake up each morning with the same feeling of excitement and adventure I had as a seventeen-year-old coming to America. I say, "Thank you, Lord! I'm heading for the Promised Land. Maybe I'll have a chance to do something about 401(k) plans after all!"

On a brisk morning in March, I return to the AMAX battlefield. I wave to the curious secretaries on the top floor of corporate headquarters where I once ran board meetings. I enter the corner office previously occupied by Ian MacGregor and Pierre Gousseland, to see Al Born. It is important to make a clean break and give up all my AMAX benefits before starting government service. I have no regrets. Even the prospect of a lower salary doesn't seem to matter because I have a higher calling.

I receive Form SF 76 from the White House requesting detailed information about my personal life. I complete the package and return it the next day. At the same time, knowing that Secretary Dole wants me to come to work right away, we put our house on the market.

We take a quick exploratory trip to Washington before making specific plans. I would like to live at the farm, which is fifty miles outside of DC, and commute, perhaps renting a one-room apartment in town. But Carol wants to keep the family together. She says, "I have a list of houses for rent near National Cathedral." Leaving Jon, age ten, and Thomas, age four, curled up in front of the television at the Quality Inn, we prowl around in the dark, checking several places.

A number of people look at our house in Greenwich. Within a few days we have a contract to sell at close to our asking price. The next weekend, with growing enthusiasm, we return to Washington and find an old townhouse for rent at 1684 Thirty-Second Street in Georgetown near Dumbarton Oaks. I love the Federal-style windows facing south and the tiny brick patio surrounded by a white fence. The living room has a wood-burning fireplace. I tell Carol, "If you want to live in Washington, this is it!" She laughs at my impulsiveness.

On Easter Sunday after we return from church, an FBI agent phones. She wants a list of thirty of my friends right away. Carol and I review our Christmas card list and give her thirty names and addresses. We congratulate each other on satisfying the request so easily. But the next day she asks for another thirty.

The pressure builds when Dad says he has heard about the FBI investigation from Miss Watson, a member of his old church in Johnson Creek. She had sponsored us for citizenship. The phone shakes in my hand. Why are they calling western New York?

The FBI turns to our neighbors and my business associates at AMAX, who were not on my list. By now I have a headache. Is it possible for me to lose the job because my wife committed suicide?

On Thursday the agent reaches her deadline. She tells me her team has interviewed thirty-five people and unearthed nothing derogatory. What a load off my mind! My spirit soars when she adds, "I'm not supposed to tell you this, but I've never heard so many positive things about anyone I've investigated."

Just as I start to relax, I run into another difficulty in the form of a questionnaire for sensitive positions from the White House counsel. It includes a question about directors of organizations that restrict membership on the basis of sex. I call Nelson Lund in the White House Counsel's office. "What should I do? I'm a director of Skull and Bones, my senior society at Yale. Even though there are no restrictions on membership in the charter, no female members have been elected to the organization since the university first admitted women in 1969."

Nelson Lund replies, "You should resign as a director immediately."

I rise to the challenge. "The president is a member!"

"He's not a director," the lawyer points out. "You can either resign now or wait until Senator Metzenbaum brings it up at your confirmation hearings." I reluctantly agree to resign. Nelson promises to report favorably on my disclosure.

His comment makes me wonder how Senator Metzenbaum feels about my appointment. As chairman of the Senate labor subcommittee, he has jurisdiction over my confirmation and undoubtedly remembers my controversial innovations to save AMAX. I don't have to wait long to find out.

That same night Rod DeArment calls. "There's been a disturbing development. Mrs. Dole has received a letter from Senator Metzenbaum objecting to your appointment because of your involvement with the AMAX pension reversions."

# Chapter Twenty-Three

## *A Hostile Senator*

The opposition of Senator Metzenbaum to my nomination drains my joy. On April 5, I sheepishly report for work as a consultant at the Labor Department. Within hours of arrival, I help draft a response from Mrs. Dole to the senator. However, without confirmation, I have no authority to discuss policy with the staff of my agency, the Pension and Welfare Benefit Administration. I don't dare mention 401(k) plans.

While I live in Georgetown, Carol remains in Greenwich until Jon and Thomas finish the school year. I wish they could be with me during this uncertainty. Christopher hears of my vulnerability. His letter from Vassar brings a lump to my throat. "After the catastrophic event of my mother dying, I closed myself off from the world. One result of this has been a superficial relationship with you. I'm going to make an effort to have a more open friendship. Dad, you should stand tall and proud. I sure as hell am, to be your son."

Because the Democrats control the Senate, I realize I need help from Democratic senators in order to be confirmed. I pay a courtesy call on Senator David Boren, a Democrat from Oklahoma and a Yale graduate. He promises to speak to Senator Metzenbaum. He adds, "Try to see him yourself as soon as possible." He invites me to ride with him from his office to the White House on the way to a ceremony in the Rose Garden.

That very same evening my secretary calls. "The president nominated you today and sent your name to the Senate."

I call Carol to share the news. "Well, at least I was nominated!"

She loyally replies, "We'll be joining you in two months."

Now I have to face the music. With great trepidation I call on Senator Metzenbaum in his dark, cavernous office. He glares at me with piercing eyes under a shock of white hair, cold and fierce in his determination to bite back pension reversions. He growls, "David, I have nothing against you personally. You're a pawn! If you return with an administration proposal about reversions that I find acceptable, you'll be confirmed the next day."

As I ride the Metroliner up to Connecticut for the weekend, I reflect on his outrageous proposition. It sounds like a violation of his Constitutional duty to give "advice and consent." The Constitution doesn't contemplate a game of political chess with presidential nominees. I never paid any attention to this kind of torture until it happened to me. I grit my teeth through well-meaning good-bye dinners hosted by Greenwich friends, wondering if this has all been for nothing.

I fly to Long Beach, California, as a powerless observer at the annual conference of my agency. Walking along the beach where I swam and sunbathed with Morganne, I remember the magical summer of 1962. I drive over to Claremont for an emotional reunion with Zee, whom I haven't seen since Bob died several years before. She no longer feels up to traveling east to visit us and lives in a retirement home decorated with photographs of Morganne. She says, "I know it's been a struggle with the children. Thank goodness for Carol."

On a sunlit day in June, the older children and I visit Morganne's grave in Putnam Cemetery in Greenwich. She was a kind, good person. I don't like to remember her suffering, but after years of confusion, I accept that her feelings of worthlessness were an illness. As the children place wild daises on her grave, I feel the sun on my back and think of her warm, open smile. I trim the grass around the stone with my hands and say a loving good-bye.

Before we uproot for Washington, Carol and I want to show the children the Statue of Liberty. Dave helps us bump Thomas's stroller up the narrow stairs inside the monument, to the crown with its distant view of Manhattan. As the children peer across the water, I remember seeing the Statue of Liberty through the fog in 1954 when I arrived as an immigrant. I didn't know then that Martin Luther King Jr. would help free me from the narrow path that Mum required. He inspired me to try to make a difference in the world, and now I'm hoping for an opportunity to do that in the government. What an incredible country it is!

In June, Carol arrives in Georgetown with Jon, Thomas, and a moving van. Christopher, who has a summer job with the moving company, unloads some of our furniture and drives off with the rest to the farm. Carol has already investigated the local public schools. At the first place she visited, she found children talking and throwing spitballs at each other while the beleaguered teacher was speaking. A secretary at her next stop warned her to arrive before nine o'clock, when they lock out the drug dealers. Shocked and disheartened, we confront the expense of private schools.

My salary in the government is $72,000 a year. Carol says, "It's peanuts!" Of course it isn't peanuts, but although it pays the rent and our living expenses, it doesn't cover the cost of two children in college, two in private school, and the mortgage on the farm. We cut back on vacations, hold on to our aging cars, and dip into the proceeds from the sale of our house in Belle Haven.

As June turns into July, I find have nothing to do. I sit at my desk in a temporary office at the Labor Department waiting for Senator Metzenbaum to remove his hold. I know only too well that after the brilliant interview with Elizabeth Dole, clearance by the FBI, and nomination by President Bush, I could still end up hanging around with no serious job. Each morning as I head for my uncertain position at the department, I put on a bold face. I knew this was going to be painful. But inside, my confidence drips away.

It dawns on me that ever since Senator Metzenbaum opposed my nomination, the staff in the front office of the Labor Department has stopped arranging courtesy calls in the Senate. They've left me hanging. I need to help myself.

In desperation I call AMAX director Harold Brown, former secretary of defense, who sends me to see Senator Christopher Dodd from Connecticut. Even though a Democrat, Senator Dodd welcomes me as a resident of his home state and agrees to introduce me at my confirmation hearing. I also call on Senator Joseph Lieberman, another Democrat, who has just been elected as the junior senator from

Connecticut. He seems quite friendly. We chat about how, in the recent election, many people in our home state split the ticket and voted for George Bush for president and Joe Lieberman for senator. He sends me off with a firm handshake and a warm smile.

I wonder where to turn next. The staff in the front office remains ominously silent. Bill Coleman, my confidant on the AMAX board, calls. "Dave, how come you're not confirmed yet?"

I reply, "Senator Metzenbaum has put a hold on my nomination."

He says cheerfully, "Look, I want you to meet some friends of mine."

He takes me to see Senators Nancy Kassenbaum and Thad Cochran and promises to speak to Senator Ted Kennedy on my behalf. His kindness strikes me as amazing. Come to think of it, so does that of the other AMAX directors, Harold Brown and President Ford. More than two years after Al Born kicked me out as corporate secretary, they have come to my aid. I hope I can live up to their expectations.

On Bill Coleman's advice, I set up my own meeting with Senator Kennedy's staff. They want to know my views on whether workers should share in any excess funds in connection with a pension restructuring. I point out that at AMAX we gave all the participants an increase in benefits. The staffers listen attentively. Kennedy, as chairman of the full Labor and Management Committee, can override Metzenbaum, who chairs only a subcommittee. Usually the chairman honors the hold of a nomination by a committee member for a reasonable period of time. But he has the power to move the nomination for a vote.

At the end of July one of Kennedy's staffers tells me, "I've informally polled the committee for the senator and found it to be fifteen to one in favor of your confirmation." The staffer adds, "He plans to schedule your markup for the first meeting of the committee after the summer recess."

A friend in the congressional liaison office at the Labor Department, explains, "You're the fortunate beneficiary of a fight between senators." Apparently, Senator Kennedy wanted a health care bill to be the only Labor Committee bill attached to budget reconciliation. Against Kennedy's wishes, Metzenbaum attached his pension reversion bill. The maneuver so angered Kennedy that he informed his colleague he intended to mark up my nomination as assistant secretary of labor. I think, *How ironic and how wonderful that the lion of the Democratic Party has chosen to move my confirmation.*

While Congress recesses, at Windsor Farm we have another family reunion attended by all thirty members of Dad and Sylvia's families. Dad, at age eighty-two, still preaches once a month at Baptist churches around Gloucester. Now he leads a Sunday worship service on the farm porch. As Sylvia pedals at the little borrowed organ, he belts out the hymns with the same power and conviction I remember from my childhood at Trinity.

For his sermon he uses another of his favorite words, "Jehovah-Jireh," which means God will provide. A gust of wind disturbs the treetops, changing the pattern of sunlight on the floor of the porch. Dad looks at his gathered family and declares, "I encourage each of you to put God first in your lives, and he will provide all your needs."

On October 4 the Labor and Management Committee approves my nomination by unanimous consent. This must have included Metzenbaum. The nomination now goes to the full Senate, where under Senate custom a single senator can delay a vote on the floor. Two days later, I learn to my chagrin he has placed another hold. How could he be so cruel?

Senator Dole speaks up. "I hope we can resolve any last-minute snags on the nomination. It's been pending for some time. I hope we can confirm the nominee today. He's a vital member of the department, and I know the secretary very much would like to have him on board."

Apparently, Bob Dole's speech does the trick because Metzenbaum lifts his hold. On Thursday, October 13, I call the Senate cloakroom and get a recorded message that says, "The nomination of David George Ball of Connecticut was confirmed." Having had so many last-minute disappointments, I can't trust my ears. I ring the number again and hand the phone to Carol, "Please listen and tell me if it's good news."

Her huge smile says it all. We hug each other in the hallway. Almost a year after the election and many months after my interview with Elizabeth Dole, I'm ready to start my new job.

# Chapter Twenty-Four

## *THE JOY AND THE CHALLENGE OF PUBLIC SERVICE*

I gaze in wonder at my new quarters in the Labor Department, the largest office I have ever had. It even has its own bathroom and shower. I can see myself jogging on the Mall in the freshness of the new day.

*The Prune Book* describes my position as one of the "one hundred toughest management and policy-making jobs in Washington," but like the sunlight flooding my desk, it gives me great joy.

The words of a hymn echo in my mind: "Morning has broken like the first morning, blackbird has spoken like the first bird. Praise for the singing! Praise for the morning! Praise for them, springing fresh from the Word!" It exactly expresses my elation in feeling that Providence has brought me to Washington to somehow fulfill the call I heard all those years ago at Yale, when that eloquent black Baptist preacher from Montgomery, Alabama, urged us to help make the world a better place.

Elizabeth Dole officiates at a large jovial gathering that includes my family, my friends from Yale and Greenwich, and Bill Coleman. Prescott Bush enjoys telling the crowd about something I had said to Beth while I was still in limbo. "The Lord wouldn't have let us sell our house in Greenwich and move to Georgetown if he didn't want me to have this job." Joke as he may, I believe it is true.

Bill Coleman steps up to speak. "Dave, you've been waiting for a long while. Now it's time for you to get to work!"

*Bill Coleman, former secretary of transportation; Elizabeth Dole,
secretary of labor; and Carol and David at David's swearing-in ceremony
at the Labor Department in 1989. (Courtesy of Howard Allen).*

I can imagine Dad in England saying, "Ebenezer." He gives the
Labor Department press release to a reporter from the *Gloucester Citizen*,
who asks for a photograph. The *Citizen* runs a story with the delightful
caption, "Bush Calls Up David."

Auntie Vera writes from Thornbury, "How proud your mother
would have been of you. I'm glad that we have such a good man in
Parliament as David George Ball." Her poignant message reminds me
my war with Mum is over. I've made my peace with her.

Not all the coverage is so friendly. Jack Anderson's column,
"Washington Merry-Go-Round" carries the headline, "Unions Regard
Bush Nominee as Pension Raider." The article says, "His appointment
is not so much a question of ability as it is philosophy. As one Senate
staffer put it, 'He certainly understands the pension area, in some
ways too well.' " My assistant thinks Senator Metzenbaum inspired the
article with the hope it would torpedo my appointment. Fortunately,
the column doesn't run until the day after I'm confirmed.

A friend suggests I thank White House Chief of Staff John Sununu for my job. According to a rumor, the first five people that Elizabeth Dole picked were individuals who had previously worked for her or Bob Dole. On discovering this, John Sununu allegedly summoned her to the White House and said, "I thought George Bush won the election, not Bob Dole." He instructed her to find people who were loyal to George Bush. Even if the rumor is true, I believe what made a personal difference was my telling Elizabeth my mother was a missionary.

As I jog on the Mall during my lunch hour, I continue to ponder the question Elizabeth asked on Valentine's Day: "What is your mission, David?" I need to be sure of my answer.

Speeding past Mr. Jefferson in his memorial, I remember how Martin Luther King Jr. quoted him in Woolsey Hall. "All men are created equal and are endowed by their creator with certain inalienable rights, that among these are life, liberty, and the pursuit of happiness." I know I can't help everybody, but maybe I can help working Americans in their pursuit of happiness by creating more financial security in their retirement.

First and foremost, as the top official in the federal government for pensions, I must enforce the Employee Retirement Income Security Act, known as ERISA, which was signed into law in 1975 by President Ford. My most important duty is to protect the employee benefits of more than seventy million people and approximately $2.3 trillion in pension assets. Indeed, the person who holds this position is known as "the pension czar."

But I have set my heart on much more than tough enforcement of the pension law. I want to find a way to help people who have no pension whatsoever. The most realistic way to accomplish this is through the 401(k) program, which is growing in popularity in the workplace.

Traditional pension plans are not working. Like cumbersome old dinosaurs, they are a dying breed and headed for trouble. Few new defined-benefit plans are created, and existing ones are being terminated. They cover fewer and fewer people. Employees who move from job to job lose most if not all of their benefits. Traditional plans also involve huge administrative costs and large premiums to the Pension Benefit Guaranty Corporation. Employers bear the investment risk, and if they get into financial difficulty they dump the liability on the government.

Unfortunately, the pension that many beneficiaries receive from the PBGC is much smaller than the pension they would have received under the abandoned plan.

I know the secretary is concerned about this problem. In my first strategy meeting with her, she said, "David, I'd like to do something about pension portability."

As my run takes me round the tidal basin to the Washington Monument, I see the Lincoln Memorial where Martin Luther King Jr. spoke about his dream. I believe the time has come to extend the 401(k) program to workers who have nothing.

401(k) plans reflect the realities of the modern workplace where workers change jobs many times during their careers. Once the contribution is made, it belongs to the workers. Unlike the uncertainty surrounding defined benefit plans, participants know exactly how much they have in their accounts. They value the opportunity to direct their own investments. Finally, just as Elizabeth prefers, the benefits are portable.

Although I championed the first large company 401(k) back in 1981, these plans have run into a roadblock. Despite their popularity with workers, many companies have hesitated to adopt them because of concern about liability for losses arising from workers' instructions. As long as we have a voluntary pension system, this fear will limit the growth of the 401(k) program.

I believe the key to removing this fear lies in clarifying the issue of *control*. We need to provide a road map that identifies the circumstances under which workers have control over their own investments and companies are relieved of liability.

Toward the end of my jog, I sit down on a bench in the small garden in front of the National Gallery and shut my eyes to listen to the water splashing in the fountain. I remember what President Bush envisioned at the Republican Convention about giving more power and opportunity to individuals. We should give employees both the responsibility and the risk for their own investment decisions. I believe this will open up 401(k) plans to millions of workers who have no pension plan at all.

Before the early-morning staff meeting, I talk with Elizabeth Dole. I say, "Madam Secretary, I'm ready to answer the question you asked at our first meeting. I want to get out a road map to encourage employers to extend 401(k) plans to workers with no pension."

"How do you propose to do that?" she asks.

"We can do it by clarifying when workers have control over their own investments. If workers have control, many companies, which previously have hesitated out of fear of liability for losses resulting from workers' instructions, will now offer plans."

"Good!" she exclaims. "You've found your mission." She beams with pleasure, just as Mum did when I told her I was going to be a minister.

Each day I wake up with a sense of wonder. I search in my filing cabinet for the photograph of me with Martin Luther King Jr. I hang it prominently in my office. It seems as if I've been preparing for this job ever since that birthday party.

On November 9, 1989, I'm moved when the Berlin Wall comes down. I remember dreading the German bombers during the war and then seeing the devastation in East Berlin when I visited in 1959. President Bush forgoes the political benefit of going to Berlin in case it makes things difficult for Gorbachev. There's a danger of a crackdown by hard-liners and intervention by the army similar to the suppression of the democratic movement in Czechoslovakia in 1968. I feel proud to work for such a skillful president.

Mrs. Dole takes about twenty members of her political staff for a planning session at the Aspen Institute on the Wye River in Maryland. She tells us her favorite book is the Bible and her favorite historical figure is Jesus Christ. How absolutely amazing! I respect her courage in speaking this way before a group of cynical political subordinates. Like her, I want to live a life of faith. But I worry too much what other people think to risk the same kind of openness.

Carol and I attend a welcoming dinner party at the Georgetown home of one of my Yale friends. A dozen neighbors crowd into the tiny dining room to raise their glasses to the new administration. After dinner, the two of us walk back up the hill in a light rain to our townhouse, holding hands like newlyweds. Church bells peal in the distance. I hear echoes of the bells of Harkness Tower and Gloucester Cathedral singing, "Going home. Going home!"

Carol delights in taking care of only her two natural children. She says, "It's like a fresh start!" She prefers a smaller, more manageable family to the chaos of seven. We resume reading our worn and dog-eared children's Bible at dinner time. On Sunday we take the boys to St. Patrick's Episcopal Church. I bow my head in a surge of warmth and gratitude for the opportunity of my new job and for Carol as my partner.

I have an idyllic summer with Carol and all five children at Windsor Farm, with me joining them on weekends. When they are back at school, though, we get another surprise. Dave calls from Castleton State College.

"Are you both on the phone? Are you sitting down?" he asks emotionally. "I want you to know I just got married."

His bride is nineteen-year-old Kari Dimick. He met Kari while negotiating with her grandmother for Castleton Village Hall for a "Prohibition Rock" Halloween party he promoted for his fellow students. Nobody showed up and he lost a lot of money. The night of the disaster, they began to fall in love and have spent the past three weeks constantly in each other's company. They plan to live on Lake Bomoseen in a rented summer cottage while Dave finishes college.

As Dave begins married life, I worry about hearings on Capitol Hill. I spend hours with my staff preparing for tricky questions. When I testify before the Senate Labor subcommittee on enforcement of the pension laws, Senator Metzenbaum goes on the attack. He opens with a hostile statement accusing me of being probusiness.

I don't get much sympathy. My predecessor, David Walker, reminds me, "President Truman used to say, 'If you want a friend in Washington, get a dog!'" Perhaps he's right. Choo Choo has died. We get a sweet-natured English cocker spaniel whom we name Staley after the Staley family at Kington Mead Farm.

Carol delights in training our new puppy on walks in Montrose Park. She relishes her freedom to enjoy the Smithsonian, the Georgetown book club, and the Republican Women's Forum, where the wives of cabinet secretaries often invite their husbands as speakers. I tease her, "You get to meet more celebrities than I." But I know we are sharing our lives more than ever before.

In the vicious partisan atmosphere, I decide to retain David Walker's deputy, Ann Combs. She has an uncanny ability to charm the unfriendly Democrats on the hill. I also have the good fortune to inherit a talented career deputy for program operations named Alan Lebowitz. The longer the political fight continues, the more grateful I become for their loyalty and support. But my strongest ally on the road map remains Elizabeth Dole. She says, "Let me know what I can do to help."

The staff in the Office of Regulations and Interpretations produces a first draft of the proposed regulation, which is over one hundred pages long. It provides an elaborate description of control and includes an extensive description of various investment options. Much of this seems unnecessary and would be better left to the marketplace. As a new man on the job, I hesitate to criticize the careful staff work, but I come to regret my timidity.

I feel honored when Beth Bush inquires whether she and Pres could stay with us during a visit to Washington, although this creates a dilemma because we don't have a spare room. We can't put the president's brother in the basement. I think the best solution is for us to spend the night at Windsor Farm and give them our master bedroom. It doesn't occur to me to extend homey hospitality by openly giving them our bed and sleeping in the basement ourselves.

*David with Secretary of Labor Elizabeth Dole*
*at the Labor Department in 1989.*

In August 1990, Iraq invades Kuwait and threatens Saudi Arabia and the world oil supply. President Bush mobilizes United States troops in the Gulf and skillfully obtains widespread support from a coalition of over thirty nations. I hope Saddam Hussein's aggression will not lead us into war. The scare guns the price of oil over forty dollars a barrel and consumer confidence falls. Americans cut back on their spending and push the economy into a recession that lasts until March.

Carol and I continue our own economic recession by driving our aging cars. Carol buys food at low bulk prices at the Price Club and children's clothes at the Junior League Thrift Shop. She takes a job as assistant business manager of St. Patrick's Episcopal School to help pay for Thomas's tuition there. We look for a less expensive house to rent. With the big mortgage on the farm and the cost of the children's tuition, our expenses vastly exceed our income. The money from the sale of our house in Greenwich dwindles fast.

In October during dinner with the family, I receive a phone call from Elizabeth Dole. She says, "David, I want you to know that tomorrow I'll announce my resignation to become president of the American Red Cross." Her news brings another twist of anxiety about my pension regulation. She's served only twenty-one months of her four-year term.

"I'm very sorry. I love working for you," I reply.

Her voice sounds as if she's smiling when she says, "I believe God is giving me an opportunity to help in another way."

At her last staff meeting on November 16, several people cry. In the midst of the gloom, her assistant walks in with a birthday cake for me. I stare at the cake, puzzled by all this attention. While everybody sings, "Happy Birthday," I wonder how to respond. Even without Mrs. Dole's support, I must persevere with the road map in the spirit of our joint ideals. I say, "Madam Secretary, thank you very much for the birthday cake and for your enthusiasm for the 401(k) program. You have lit such a candle as shall never be put out."

After the meeting, I discover a story in the *Washington Post* that explains some of the tears. It carries the headline, "Labor Department Exodus Expected," and predicts that "the whole crew" with specific ties to one or the other Dole will go. However it continues, "David Ball is believed secure and happy in his job. Politically, unlike many others in the department, Ball's ties are with Bush, through the president's brother in Connecticut."

We take Jon and Thomas to a Christmas reception at the White House. While Carol chats with George and Barbara Bush, and Jonathan shakes hands with the president, Thomas pets Millie, their English springer spaniel. From my position by the Christmas tree in the Blue Room, I see Mr. Jefferson looking at me. I give him a nod as I think of my resolve to get out the pension regulation.

I press on with the draft proposal. We obtain clearance from the solicitor of labor and the secretary's office. Now we must get approval from the White House. Alan Lebowitz and I meet with the staff of the Office of Management and Budget, known as OMB. They have a lot of questions.

Several weeks later, disaster strikes. OMB rejects our draft as cumbersome and unworkable. Alan Lebowitz and Bob Doyle, director of the Office of Regulations and Interpretations, come to my office in dismay. Bob protests, "We should bag the whole thing."

After they leave I reflect on the collapse of my dream. With Elizabeth Dole about to leave, the timing couldn't be worse. But I then remember Martin Luther King Jr. pushing forward after the catastrophe at the Pettus Bridge. I'm not going to "bag" anything. I'm going to carry on.

I study the one-hundred-page draft and conclude OMB has a point. It is too long and very confusing. We only need a few pages to define meaningful control. First, workers must have adequate information. Second, they must have the opportunity to diversify their investments. Third, they must have regular opportunities to give instructions. If we focus on these ingredients, I believe we can come up with a dramatically simpler regulation.

This is my mission and I'm not giving up. But will I get it through without the support of Elizabeth Dole?

# Chapter Twenty-Five

## *"The Most Significant Thing to Affect the Pension Industry in Years"*

I decide to test my idea for a dramatically simpler regulation on John Baitsel, a Labor Policy Association friend, who is a leader in the two major pension-trade organizations. He thinks they will work. Now I must confront my staff.

I inform Alan Lebowitz that I want to revise the road map. We should keep it uncomplicated with three broad requirements to give workers independent, meaningful control over the investment of their pension dollars. First, participants must have sufficient information to make informed investment decisions. Second, they must be able to choose from a broad range of investment alternatives so they can diversify. This means employers must provide at least three investment vehicles, each having materially different characteristics of risk and return. Third, workers must be able to give investment instructions with a frequency that is appropriate in light of the market volatility of the investment options, which in many cases will mean at least once every quarter. Compliance with these requirements will relieve fiduciaries from liability for investment losses resulting from participants' control over the assets in their accounts.

Alan gasps, "We'll have to throw out dozens of pages of the draft!"

But I'm not backing off. Bob Doyle and the staff start to outline the new road map.

199

I worry about the 401(k) program while I attend weekly meetings at the White House as a member of the president's working group on health care. We all fear that any legislative proposal on health care will be squashed. Thank goodness we don't need congressional approval of the road map.

My agency brings several lawsuits against companies that have purchased annuities for their pension plans from a collapsed life insurer, even though there was reason for those companies to suspect that these were not the "safest available" annuities. The litigation generates a lot of interest in the media and on Capitol Hill. I campaign on ABC and NBC television and testify before the Senate Labor Committee. Senator Metzenbaum compliments me on bringing the lawsuits, but asks, "Why has it taken so long?"

A member of my staff reports a troubling rumor circulating on the Hill. Senator Metzenbaum has hired a full-time consultant to investigate my background. This new threat hisses in the back of my mind like the fuse of a bomb about to explode. I remember Corporal May dealing with unexploded bombs during the war. He said, "I try not to think about it!"

It's easy to forget Senator Metzenbaum on January 16 when the woman sitting next to Carol at a performance of *Othello* in the Folger Theater whispers, "The bombing has started!" Congress has authorized the president to use force to implement UN resolutions instructing Saddam Hussein to withdraw from Kuwait. On the way home, we listen to news reports on the radio. Then we watch the bombing of Baghdad on CNN. It seems so impersonal, but it must be as terrifying for the little children in Baghdad as it was for me crawling under my bed in fear of German bombers during World War II.

A few days later the president is over an hour late when the Marine Band plays "Hail to the Chief" and he walks into the Great Hall to swear in Lynn Martin, a former congresswoman, as the new secretary of labor. Mrs. Martin says, "I'm grateful that on this fateful day, the president made time to carry on the daily business of government." At the reception afterward, I learn he has given Saddam Hussein until Saturday noon to get out of Kuwait. Fortunately for me, the new secretary finds time to invite me to continue as pension czar.

The land war starts on February 25, and two days later the invading Iraqi forces retreat. President Bush orders a cease-fire. Although sadly, the Iraqi death toll is huge, there are few coalition casualties. On March 6 Congress calls a joint session to congratulate the president on the victory. His approval rating soars to 91 percent. The Democrats try to divert attention toward the economy and the recession caused by the war, but his chances for reelection seem high.

Carol and I attend a garden party at the British embassy in honor of Queen Elizabeth's birthday. What a thrill! With Carol on my arm looking glamorous in a new hat with green and white trim, I walk proudly up Massachusetts Avenue past a statue of Winston Churchill making his familiar V-for-victory salute, the salute I copied as a child in Gloucester watching the convoys heading for the invasion of Normandy. We stroll over the grass in the June sunshine, around white tents brimming with cucumber sandwiches and tea cakes, to inspect the roses blooming along the wall of the Georgian mansion.

We pass Jesse Jackson and his wife standing alone next to a table under a tent. Jesse participated in the 1965 march led by Dr. King from Selma to Montgomery. We go over and introduce ourselves. Carol says, "I've heard so much about you. It's great to finally meet you in person."

We chat for a few minutes. His wife confides, "Jesse leads such a hectic life, it's only on rare occassions like this that we have a chance to be together."

A member of the embassy staff perched on the roof spots the queen's limosine and raises the royal standard. Trumpeters in white pith helmets announce her arrival at the embasssy. Thirty minutes later the Royal Marine Band beats retreat. There she is, at the top of the steps of the grand entrance with Vice President Dan Quayle. A snowplow of Royal Navy officers dressed in white protects her as she mingles with us in the garden. She gives Carol a beautiful smile and shakes the hand of the lady standing next to her. That's as close as we get. Never mind; I feel honored. As a schoolboy in England, I never even got a glimpse of the queen.

As we forge ahead with the road map, Bob Doyle from the Office of Regulations and Interpretations asks, "Should we provide relief for employers from liability for investments in company stock?" I know from my experience at AMAX that employers like to use company stock in 401(k) plans because it encourages an identity of interest between employees and shareholders.

I reply, "Yes, we should include company stock. But we must also insist on the right protections for employees."

Loyal soldier Bob, who once wanted to "bag the whole thing," returns with the necessary language. We've struggled over this for three years. Now we need to move. I concentrate on the draft with the same single-mindedness as when getting the ball out of the scrum in rugby. I pass it back quickly with my approval.

After circulating our proposal to other agencies, I receive unexpected comments from the Securities and Exchange Commission. Two commissioners want to impose their own disclosure requirements on 401(k) plans. I object strenuously. We have already provided for sufficient information to make informed investment decisions, and the addition of SEC prospectuses would end up confusing people. The SEC has no experience in the workplace or in administering pension plans.

I send the new draft over to OMB and hold my breath. To my great joy, they clear the proposal. I send a status report to President Ford. He replies with a note of encouragement. What a blessing to have the support of the president who signed ERISA into law.

There is still the hurdle of public hearings which could result in more changes and delay. Time is against me.

The Democrats continue to hammer President Bush for the recession and say he has no domestic agenda. His standing is sliding downward in the polls. If he loses the election, the new draft may not see the light of day.

Besides fearing for the regulation, I worry that my glorious position may not last beyond January 1993. I think about this when my old boss, now *Sir* Ian MacGregor after serving as head of British Steel and British Coal, invites Carol and me to dinner at the Watergate Hotel. As chairman of the American subsidiary of Trust Houses Forte, he has just purchased the hotel. I get a buzz when I walk in and he says, "Hello, Mr. Secretary!"

"Hello, Mr. Chairman," I reply.

I feel sure he has a purpose in wanting to see me, and he does. In a friendly schmooze after dinner, he inquires, "How would you like to be general counsel of my company, headquartered in San Diego?"

Carol and I consider his offer while on vacation on the West Coast. Perhaps I should bail out while I still have a chance to land a good job. It sounds tempting, but am I going to abandon my call to service? I remember how after the march from Selma, Martin Luther King Jr. said that he was not going to quit. I'll stick with it no matter how bad the president's prospects.

Our ready cash has gone. I don't know where to turn. I surrender a split-dollar life insurance policy acquired at AMAX in order to pay next term's tuition for Debby and Jon. I pray, "Lord, help me to finish the job."

Our lives are still haunted by the past. Debby, returning from her junior year studying in Australia, finds it difficult to put together a realistic picture of her mother. She wants to learn more. I dig out copies of Morganne's letters to Blanche, which Blanche, thoughtful to the last, instructed her executor to pass on to me after her death. Debby seems relieved to read her mother's own words. She says, "I had an intelligent, caring, loving mom. It's a weight off my soul."

*David and Carol (holding Thomas and their puppy Staley) with Christopher, Jon, Dave, and Debby at Windsor Farm in 1990.*

On discovering how important Morganne's letters are to Debby, I send copies to Dave and Chris, together with a photo of Morganne sitting proudly with them in front of the house that we built on Buckfield Lane. I want to open a dialogue that includes everything I can remember about Morganne, her laughter and gentle humility, as well her depression and death. They all need this information to speed their recovery. Morganne's mother Zee also asks for copies.

As I talk and write about my glimmering girl, some of the dark shadows escape and disappear. Now, by the grace of God, I'm free to share my story.

Carol and I visit Zee and her friend Harriett at their retirement home in Claremont, California. As Harriett and Carol walk to the dining room, they meet some other residents. Harriett hesitates and says to Carol, "I'm not sure what to call you!"

Carol says, "Call me Zee's stepdaughter-in-law."

Later Zee writes, "Unlike the old fairy tales, I believe that sometimes, in rare instances, there can be happy endings. It gives me deep pleasure that you, who have suffered and worried so much about my grandchildren, should give me the privilege of calling you my stepdaughter. We have refuted the stepmother stereotype, just as you did long ago with Dave, Chris, and Debby. For me this is a form of benediction."

The family grows when Dave's wife, Kari, gives birth to a son, whom they name David III. They bring him to Trinity Church in Upperville on Boxing Day for his christening. Debby reads part of the sacrament, and Jon serves as acolyte. Thomas pours the water for the font.

My assistant for public affairs, Hal Glassman, tells me an investigative reporter named Frank Greve, for the Knight-Ridder newspaper chain, has started snooping around the cafeteria at the Labor Department, sparking conversations with lower-ranking career employees about me. Hal says, "He talks to the union representative and to the troublemakers."

"Why let him in the cafeteria?" I ask.

He replies grimly, "We can't keep him out!"

A few weeks later, a friend from law school who knew Morganne receives a call from Frank Greve, as does Pierre Gousseland, the former chief executive of AMAX. The investigation makes me jumpy. Carol asks, "Who's he going to call next?"

I get even edgier at a White House briefing when Boyden Gray, counsel to the president, says, "Ethics are the weapon of choice in destroying someone politically." Searching my behavior for anything questionable, I know I refused to let anyone dealing with the department pay for lunch or dinner. I recused myself from one policy issue remotely involving AMAX. I've vigorously enforced the law.

Finally, Frank Greve breaks cover. Hal Glassman says, "He wants an interview. I recommend you see him."

As I prepare anxiously with Hal, I ask, "What exactly does Greve want to know?" I tell Hal about Morganne's suicide. I mention Skull and Bones, my senior society at Yale. The president is a member.

On the day of the interview, Greve marches boldly into my office. I wonder if I have been set up for a bonfire like the conflagration on Guy Fawkes Day in my childhood. Did an unfriendly politician like Senator Metzenbaum inspire this investigation as a desperate last-minute attempt to sabotage my work on the new pension regulation? The timing looks suspicious—just before I testify at a hearing of the House Subcommittee on the Aging. I confess to Hal, "I'm scared I will embarass the president."

On February 2, the headline in the *Philadelphia Inquirer* screams, "Heat is on US Pension Watchdog." The article focuses on the enormous task in monitoring, with just a few hundred employees, the nation's 900,000 pension plans. But, to my relief, there is little personal in the attack.

Debby arrives unheralded at my office, so I invite her to hear me testify before the House Subcommittee on the Aging. Her laughter in the car distracts and comforts me. Frank Greve sits in the back row of the hearing room, and the crowd seems unusually large. The chairman of the committee, Representative William Hughes, a Democrat, fires questions about enforcement. Nobody mentions the proposed regulation governing 401(k) plans.

When the chairman hammers down the gavel to conclude the hearing, I wipe my hand over my sweaty forehead in satisfaction. Frank Greve stalks out shaking his head.

Debby volunteers to serve with the Peace Corps in Niger, West Africa. As Carol drives her to Dulles Airport, she says, "I'm grateful for everything you've done for me." After her departure, I miss Debby's cheerful laughter and enthusiasm for the farm. I wish I'd given her all the time and attention she needed when she was young. Once a week I write to Niger, and every day when I jog on the Mall, I stop to pray for her.

Although the Democrats criticize President Bush for having no domestic agenda, they can't stop me moving forward with public hearings at the Department of Labor on the road map. Fortunately, the witnesses from the business, insurance, and pension communities step up to support the proposal. What a load off my mind! Now I need to perfect the language and obtain final clearance. I race to finish the job before the election.

During a trip to Chicago for the annual managers' conference of my agency, I decide to attend chapel with my brother's son-in-law, Rick, who represents the third generation of our family to attend Moody Bible Institute. He startles me with the news that Dr. Joseph Stowell, the president of Moody, would like to see me. Dr. Stowell confides, "We have a problem with our pension plan." He calls in his general counsel, Marvin Beckman, to give me the details. I offer to look into it.

After I help resolve his pension problem, Marvin Beckman invites me to a lunch at the Sheraton Washington Hotel for over a thousand people attending the annual convention of National Religious Broadcasters. The speakers include President Bush and Billy Graham. One of the guests of honor is Elizabeth Dole. The president describes how prayer and his belief in God helped him during the War in the Gulf.

Dr. Stowell presides. After recognizing the other government officials, he mentions that I attended Moody and asks me to stand. I notice Elizabeth Dole beaming in my direction. When I rise joyfully to my feet, it seems as if the disparate people in my life have unexpectedly come together to bless my vocation. My childhood calling to the ministry has converged with a call to serve in the government. Like Elizabth Dole, I have a sense of mission about public service.

The money from the sale of the house in Greenwich has gone. In desperation I borrow from my Federal Thrift Plan account to pay for Debby's last year in college and to buy Carol a more roadworthy secondhand car. Trying to remember I'm blessed to have the farm at all, I reluctantly increase its mortgage.

In England, Ruth and Jim are struggling to not lose their home as a result of the collapse of Jim's business in the recession. Ruth now tutors for Oxford University and writes children's books. Increasingly, I think of her as a kindred spirit and treasure her friendship. I share with her on the phone my frustration at another delay in the publication of the road map. "It would be really grim to get this close and not finish the job."

The president's standing in the polls sinks lower. Although the economy started to expand in March 1991, the recovery is not visible to the man and woman on the street. The jobless rate, which lags behind broader turning points, keeps rising through June 1992, when it hits 7.8 percent. Then, to make matters worse, Ross Perot crashes into the race, threatening to split the Republican vote.

As the political situation becomes more ominous, Thomas, now eight, touches some poison oak. His face swells up, distorted, leaving only slits for his eyes. He says, "Dad, my face looks like the Phantom of the Opera." Just when I need it, Thomas makes me laugh.

I accept an invitation to return to Moody to speak at morning chapel. Twenty-two hundred young people jam the sanctuary where I once worshiped as a student. Moved, I tell them about Dad, who attended Moody from 1928 to 1931. "His influence on my life has not been so much through his preaching as through his example. He lives for the glory of God and the good of others. His motto is loving-kindness."

After chapel dozens of students gather around me in the front of the sanctuary with questions about my career. I feel elated at their friendliness and curiosity. One girl confides, "I'm not sure about my calling."

I reassure her, "For those of us who do not end up as ministers or missionaries, we can be confident that the Lord needs Christian laymen and laywomen."

The election speeds toward me like a gathering storm, but miraculously, three weeks before election day, the regulation appears in the Federal Register under my signature. Just to see the road map in printed form gives me joy.

I lean over my desk at the Labor Department to check the stories in the newspapers. A report in the *Washington Post* on October 14, 1992, carries the headline, "Workers to Gain More Pension-Dollar Say." The

*New York Times* quotes a financial expert saying, "This is the most significant thing to affect the pension industry in years."

I whisper, "Thank you, Lord."

The thirty-two page regulation enacts the president's promise to give more power and opportunity to individuals. I think, *It's part of his domestic legacy. He should talk about it in the campaign.*

Someone in the campaign gets the same idea. Two days later I receive an urgent phone call at home from Steve Hoffman, assistant secretary for Public Affairs. He says, "David, I'm at the debate between the president and Governor Clinton in Richmond. It starts in forty-five minutes. Please explain the new reg. The president might want to mention it."

As I wait in my office for the election results, I reflect on my dream of a 401(k) program at AMAX in 1981. Now that employers have a road map to follow, I believe many workers, who would otherwise have nothing, will enjoy a financially secure retirement. I glance in gratitude at the familiar photograph of Martin Luther King Jr. near the door.

But the election news is bad. George Bush loses with 38 percent of the popular vote. Ross Perot receives 19 percent. Bill Clinton wins with 43 percent. What am I going to do now?

# Chapter Twenty-Six

## *EPIPHANY ON A ROOF*

I shudder at the prospect of losing my job. Brooding in the growing darkness of my office, I stare at a letter from President Ford. "You should be very proud of your success in strengthening the integrity of the private pension system." With an unsteady hand, I pick up a personal note from President Bush that says, "Thanks for your honorable service." Distracted by my anxiety, I listen to a message from Bill Coleman. "Dave, you have made a tremendous contribution to how pensions should be handled."

I try to let their words cheer me, but can't avoid my shattered feelings. Even the commendation of Bill Coleman doesn't help.

Why is it that after fulfilling my dream of political achievement I don't have Martin Luther King Jr.'s peace of mind? I'm afraid of being relegated to obscurity. The good luck of some appointees in landing spectacular jobs after government service torments me.

The managing partner of Williams Mullen, a small law firm in Richmond, Virginia, has offered me a position. I would start a new office in Washington. I certainly need the money, but the job is not as grand as I hoped. Should I take it or look for something more impressive?

I jog on the Mall, stopping at the garden in front of the National Gallery to pray for guidance. I zip up my jacket against the bitter wind that churns up dead leaves. As I turn at the Lincoln Memorial to follow the bank of the Potomac, the clouds occasionally part, making the river sparkle. When I reach the tidal basin, I run up the steps and salute Mr. Jefferson. He looks at me calmly, perhaps with compassion for my overwrought state.

The next day, we drive out to Windsor Farm for a hunt breakfast that includes many of our friends in the government. The weather turns bleak with rain and floods. Over one hundred people cram into our front hall and living room to drink hot spiced cider or wassail. A great fire, banked high with logs, flames in the hearth. I laugh and smile but nothing seems certain or safe.

Afterward, I wander to my desk in the library to reread a confident letter from Dad. "Providence is still in control, and soon you will see what God has in store for you."

*Jonathan and Arlene, Carol and David, with Sylvia, Dad*
*and Staley on the porch at Windsor Farm in 1992*

With her usual foresight, Carol has suggested unusual plans for New Year's Eve to provide distraction. She wants to attend Renaissance Weekend in Hilton Head, South Carolina. She says, "It will be mostly Democrats, but they want more Republicans." On December 29, Carol, Christopher, Jon, Thomas, and I arrive at the big event. As Republicans, we are definitely in the minority. The Democrats glory in the recapture of the White House after twelve years out of power.

Chris, Jon, and Thomas decide to join a football game on the beach. President-elect Bill Clinton and Chelsea play on the other side.

That night as we go in to dinner, Bill Clinton greets us at the door. I shake his hand and say, "Since I went to Yale, I'm proud you'll be our fourth president."

"Who are the other three?" he asks.

"William Howard Taft, Gerald Ford, and George Bush."

He laughs. "All Republicans! So I'm the first Democrat!"

I shake his hand, but inside I hurt. He's in and I'm out!

The children receive an invitation to a special lunch to get to know a celebrity. Jon chooses the Olympic track star Edwin Moses and arrives early to sit near the guest of honor. The second person to arrive is Chelsea Clinton, who sits next to Jon. She tells him she doesn't know any kids her age in Washington. Jon reassures her. "It was hard when I first moved from Greenwich, but I did make friends. Now I really love Washington." They hang around together for the special activities organized for the youngsters.

When we return home, Jon says, "I'd like to go to the inauguration." I wonder if he has developed a crush on Chelsea.

I think about Jon at the next Labor Department staff meeting when an assistant secretary points out that the roof of the building overlooks the stage at the Capitol where the ceremony takes place. The Secret Service plans to cordon off the area around the Capitol for security reasons, but he offers any of us who are interested General Services Administration passes, providing access for construction workers servicing a television network.

I tell Carol about the passes, but add, "It won't be a celebration for me."

She insists, "I think you should take your son."

Early in the morning of January 20, Jon and I put on red flannel shirts and blue jeans. With the help of our special passes, we get through two police checkpoints. Although the Labor Department has closed for the day, I park in my regular space for the last time. When we climb the stairs, we discover NBC has built a small temporary studio at the edge of the roof facing the Capitol. Inside the studio we see Bryant Gumbel, star of *The Today Show*, interviewing an official about the history of the inauguration. We have an excellent view of President Bush, Bill Clinton, and Chelsea.

I look at my watch, which reads 11:40 AM. Pitying myself, I say to Jon, "Only twenty more minutes, and I won't be assistant secretary of labor."

I don't ask for or expect a response, but Jon replies, "Dad, you ought to be glad you have that offer from Williams Mullen."

Startled, I look at him. He's right.

Something shifts in me. Sunlight floods the crowd waiting for the swearing-in ceremony, but I'm seeing my whole life.

Mum dedicated baby David to the Lord's service, and as in a tidal wave I was swept toward the ministry. She tried to make me an answer to the secrets that tormented her by showing the world she raised a wonderful minister. In the beginning I wanted to please Mum.

Martin Luther King Jr. helped free me from the rigid course she decreed. He showed me I could serve God outside the church door. I vowed to help make the world a better place as a lawyer. After many years of striving, I even had a chance to serve the country. But I failed the Lord many times. I cared too much about the approval of others. This personal demon was there in my desire for social status at Yale and in Greenwich and in my hunger for more responsibility at AMAX. In the government I craved recognition.

Now I see how God provided despite my devices and desires. He took good care of me when those German bombers flew over our Gloucester home. He was with me in the safety of Kington Mead Farm and Moody and Nick's friendship at Yale.

God was with me in the joy with Morganne, and my parents' support when she died. Night after night I fell on my knees to ask him for help. His grace was present when Carol chose to take on my damaged family and stick with us.

Once again in the blackness when I lost my job I took my problem to the Lord. I found comfort in prayer and the opportunity to make a new beginning in public service. God's grace was there in my interview with Elizabeth Dole and the realization of my calling.

I bask in that grace today in the gift of my children and the loving-kindness of Jonathan, Ruth, and Dad. God's love abides in daily forgiveness of sin. It is my rock, the ever-present refuge when I pray.

In front of the Capitol, the new president puts his hand on a Bible to take the oath of office. A verse I learned in childhood comes back: "The Kingdom of God is within." Suddenly, my heart sings louder and stronger than on tap day at Yale. Why worry about an impressive job? It doesn't matter what other people think—whether it's Mum or anyone else.

As the president speaks, I too make a commitment. Whatever life's circumstances, I will trust that Providence is in control.

Ebenezer!

# EPILOGUE

I will always be grateful to President George H. W. Bush for the opportunity to serve at such a critical time for the pension industry. When I began my law practice at Williams Mullen, I continued to promote the 401(k) program. In a story about the demise of old-fashioned defined benefit plans on May 13, 1993, the *Washington Post* quoted me saying, "Puzzled by the complexity of pension plans, employees seem to appreciate 401(k) plans more because they are easy to understand, provide them with the freedom to make investment choices, and can be taken with them when they switch jobs."

The road map fostered a revolution. While the number of workers in traditional pension plans continued to drop, 401(k) plans soared to take their place. By 2005 the popular new plans covered 47 million participants and $2.4 trillion in assets (see appendix).

Coverage continued to surge following the 2006 Pension Protection Act, which encourages employers to enroll workers in 401(k) plans automatically and to use target-date retirement funds and other diversified investment portfolios as the default option. Automatic plan features help workers save enough for retirement and improve diversification. Target-date funds hold a broad mix of investments and become more conservative over time. However, workers can still opt out of these employer-directed moves.

The global economic crisis that began in 2008 hit pension plans hard. Unfortunately many defined benefit plans were not adequately funded. Several companies with these plans went bankrupt and left pensioners with reduced pensions from the PBGC. To make matters worse, the PBGC, which was already in the red, faced ominous demands that it assume liability for underfunded multiemployer pension plans and underfunded state and municipal plans (see "Washington and Your Retirement," *Wall Street Journal*, June 9, 2010, p. A15). Some financially strapped state and municipal governments are considering replacing traditional pension plans with a 401(k) style plan (see "States Mull Shift in Worker Pensions," *Wall Street Journal*, 3/1/11, p. A4).

The economic downturn also caused some companies with 401(k) plans to temporarily suspend matching contributions. The challenge for workers in (k) plans was to continue to maximize their own contributions and purchase new shares while prices were low, so they could take advantage of appreciation as markets recovered.

In 2009 the 401(k) program also confronted radical proposals to replace the popular plans with a government-run pension system. Ironically, the main objection appeared to be that it allows workers to control their investment decisions. However, this is the very ingredient that makes (k) plans so so effective. I believe workers should be free to control their own investments, and they should be responsible. Intervention by the government should never become so great that it removes this personal responsibility.

As a practical matter, despite the financial crisis, participants remained attacheded to their 401(k)s. A study of three thousand households by the Investment Company Institute showed that 95 percent of participants in defined contribution plans kept making contributions during the severe economic downturn (see "Survey Says Households Stick With 401(k)s", *Wall Street Journal*, January 9, 2010, p. B2). Only 2.6 percent took withdrawals and 1.3 percent took hardship withdrawals. Ninety percent of the households had a favorable view of 401(k) plans (ibid.). As companies became confident about the sustainability of the economic recovery they began to reinstate matching contributions (see "The 401(k) Match, It's Coming Back," *Washington Post*, April 11, 2010, p. G1).

By the end of 2009, as a resutlt of a resurgent stock market and ongoing contributions, the average (k) plan balance enjoyed a significant rebound (see "401(k)s' Bear Market Bruises are Healing," *Wall Street Journal*, April 4, 2010, p. C5). Today the 401(k) program with tax-deferred growth and a company match continues to provide the best tools to keep workers' retirement on track.

The reasons for the attachment of workers to their 401(k) plans are clear. Once any contribution is made, it belongs to the workers. Unlike traditional defined benefit plans, workers know exactly how much they have in their accounts. It is their property, which they can take with them if they change jobs, manage as they see fit, and bequeath to their heirs.

Of course, the financial crisis dramatized the need for prudence.

Here's what I recommend. As long-term investors, participants should diversify broadly over different securities and different asset types. They can accomplish this by investing in low-cost total US stock market index funds, total international stock market index funds, and total bond market index funds. Their asset allocation should reflect their time horizon, risk tolerance, and long-term goals. Once a year they should rebalance their portfolio to the asset mix that is right for them.

The 401(k) program, which covered only a few thousand workers when I championed the first large plan at AMAX in 1981, has grown to over seventy million participants. It has proved its value in a great fiscal trial by fire. It remains the best way in a voluntary pension system to provide financial security for workers in retirement. I believe as the economy strengthens, more companies will offer plans and many more workers will be able to enjoy pension benefits for the first time.

It's thanks, in part, to Martin Luther King Jr.

The reality of my epiphany on the roof of the Labor Department could not be achieved instantly. Struggling to meet the cost of college and private school for my two youngest children, I once again increased the mortgage on the farm. I felt an unbearable pressure to bring in business for the new Washington office of Williams Mullen, although I never wanted to be a salesman. Sometimes I forgot that Providence was in control.

Eventually, I accepted the inevitable. To provide for the future, we had to let the farm go. It was hard for all of us, but fortunately, Jonathan and Arlene had already decided to be near Arlene's aging parents.

On my retirement in 1998, Carol and I moved to Williamsburg, Virginia, where Jon, and later Thomas, attended the College of William and Mary. Dave started a pizza business in the Green Mountain State. After graduate school at the University of Virginia, Chris launched a career in financial information systems. Debby prepared for the ministry at Union Theological Seminary. As Dad prophesied, my children, who kept me humble while they were growing up, are now a source of happiness and blessing.

My modest income comes primarily from the savings in 401(k) plans at my various jobs. After nurturing the family for many years, Carol has used the talent that got her accepted by Harvard Business School to help people with the financial and personal issues involved in buying or selling their homes. I feel blessed to have her as my partner and best friend.

Until he died at age ninety-four, Dad enjoyed an incredible twenty-year honeymoon with Sylvia, and when he was no longer able to travel to America, I began regular quarterly visits to see him in Gloucester. At the same time, I had the joy of visiting my sister, Ruth, and dear Auntie Vera at Kington Mead Farm.

In 2008, Carol, Jon, and I flew out to Honolulu to share in Debby's service of ordination as a minister of the United Church of Christ. She is a chaplain for a retirement community in Honolulu. I reflected on the irony and beauty of Mum's granddaughter choosing the vocation that was not right for me.

Spiritually, Mum and I are at peace, but her energy and determination are still ingrained in me, mostly for the good, I hope.

Martin Luther King Jr., who helped free me from Mum's control, continues to be an inspiration. The photograph of me helping him cut his birthday cake at Yale stands in a place of honor in my home. It reminds me to reach out to others.

I am not a minister, but I love to read the lesson and to celebrate communion with the good people at Bruton Parish Church. Prayer is at the center of my life. By the grace of God, I've arrived at where I started and know the place for the first time.

Whenever I hear Dvorak's *New World Symphony*, I think of the bells of Harkness Tower at Yale. "Going home. Going home." The road from Gloucester has led me back where I began.

*In carriage, David's sister, Ruth Dowley, her husband James, David, and Carol with Christopher's son Ian. In front, Nicole and Jonathan Ball with their son Alexander, Deborah, Christopher, Kelly, Thomas, David Jr.'s wife Kari, and David Jr. at Colonial Williamsburg in 2010. (Courtesy of Christie Buie)*

# APPENDIX

## PENSION SHIFT

The number of people participating in 401(k) plans grew steadily from the first plans in 1981 until 2005, while the number of participants in traditional plans continued to drop.

### Active Participants in Traditional & 401(k) Plans

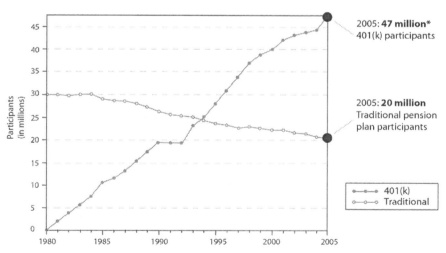

2005: **47 million***
401(k) participants

2005: **20 million**
Traditional pension plan participants

SOURCE: Department of Labor, Employee Benefit Security Administration private pension plan bulletin historical tables.

* From Investment Company Institute as reported in the Washington Post, 4/22/07, p.F4.

Following the effective date of the new regulation in 1994, the growth rate for 401(k) plans accelerated rapidly.

## 401(k) Contributions

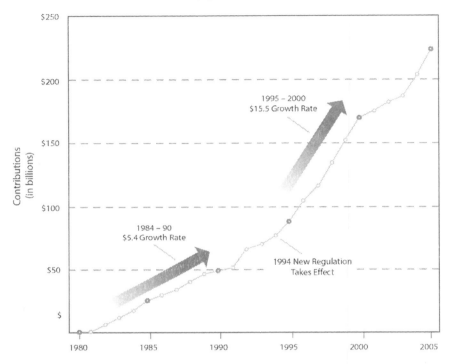

SOURCE: Department of Labor, Employee Benefit Security Administration private pension plan bulletin historical tables.

# ACKNOWLEDGMENTS

I am indebted to many people for their advice, assistance, and encouragement: John and Dorothy Ogden, Dick and Anne Lindgren, Marvin Beckman, Jean Blackall, Mark Oppenheimer, Tom Guinzburg, Tom Ross, Greg Zorthian, Paul Capron, the Rt. Reverend Herman Hollerith, Arlene Bloomer, Bruce Smith, Bill Kafes, David Holbrook, Lauren Schaeffer, Jim Ottaway, Keith Pattison, the Reverend Canon Jim Fenhagen, Al Puryear, Jack Willis, Bob Giegengack, Fred and Ellie Ernst, Larry Bogert, Rob Northrup, Roger and Hazel Staley, Holly Holbrook, Dorothy Anderson, Clayton Westland, Burt Meyer, David Leonhardt, Jack Lott, the Reverend Sidney Lovett, Dick Loos, and Jim Livingston.

My brother, Jonathan, labored through many drafts and helped keep alive my memory of our adventures together. From the start I have benefited from the insight, skill, and patience of my sister, Ruth. She has read, reread, and helped me edit many drafts of this book.

But most of all I am grateful to my wife, Carol, and my children, Dave, Chris, Debby, Jon, and Thomas for letting me share their story and for making many suggestions to improve the narrative.

# About the Author

The son of a Baptist minister and a missionary, David Ball grew up in the midst of rationing and bombing in wartime England. He came to America in 1954 to take the pastors' course at Moody Bible Institute in Chicago. Later as a scholarship student at Yale, he invited the relatively unknown Martin Luther King Jr. to speak at a lecture series he had organized. Inspired by King's example and interested in politics, he wanted to make a positive difference in people's lives.

Instead of the ministry, David's quest led him to a Wall Street law firm. He became interested in helping workers who changed jobs and were unable to take their pensions with them. In 1981 as an executive at AMAX, Inc., he championed the first 401(k) plan adopted by a large industrial company.

When President George H. W. Bush nominated him as assistant secretary of labor in 1989, David fulfilled his dream by getting out a road map to open up the revolutionary 401(k) program. Today over 70 million Americans have 401(k) plans.

CPSIA information can be obtained at www.ICGtesting.com
Printed in the USA
BVOW071331030112

279707BV00001B/3/P